# Better Homes and Gardens®

## celebrate the SEASON 2005

Meredith® Books
Des Moines, Iowa

Better Homes and Gardens®

# Celebrate the Season® 2005

Editor: Vicki Christian
Contributing Editor: Jilann Severson
Contributing Food and Wine Editor/Writer: Winifred Moranville
Contributing Recipe Editor: Joyce Trollope
Contributing Art Director/Graphic Designer: Marisa Dirks
Copy Chief: Terri Fredrickson
Publishing Operations Manager: Karen Schirm
Book Production Managers: Pam Kvitne, Marjorie J. Schenkelberg, Rick von Holdt, Mark Weaver
Contributing Copy Editor: Judy Friedman
Contributing Proofreaders: Becky Danley, Gretchen Kauffman, Donna Segal
Indexer: Jana Finnegan
Editorial Assistants: Cheryl Eckert, Kaye Chabot
Edit and Design Production Coordinator: Mary Lee Gavin

## Meredith® Books

Executive Director, Editorial: Gregory H. Kayko
Executive Director, Design: Matt Strelecki
Senior Editor/Group Manager: Jan Miller
Senior Associate Design Director: Ken Carlson

Publisher and Editor in Chief: James D. Blume
Editorial Director: Linda Raglan Cunningham
Executive Director, New Business Development: Todd M. Davis
Executive Director, Sales: Ken Zagor
Director, Operations: George A. Susral
Director, Production: Douglas M. Johnston
Director, Marketing: Amy Nichols
Business Director: Jim Leonard

Vice President and General Manager: Douglas J. Guendel

## Better Homes and Gardens® Magazine

Editor in Chief: Karol DeWulf Nickell
Deputy Editor, Home Design: Oma Blaise Ford
Deputy Editor, Food and Entertaining: Nancy Wall Hopkins

## Meredith Publishing Group

President: Jack Griffin
Executive Vice President: Bob Mate
Vice President, Corporate Solutions: Michael Brownstein
Vice President, Creative Services: Ellen de Lathouder
Vice President, Manufacturing: Bruce Heston
Vice President, Finance and Administration: Karla Jeffries
Consumer Product Associate Marketing Director: Steve Swanson
Consumer Product Marketing Manager: Wendy Merical
Business Manager: Darren Tollefson
Database Project Director: Chuck Howell

## Meredith Corporation

Chairman and Chief Executive Officer: William T. Kerr

In Memoriam: E. T. Meredith III (1933-2003)

All of us at Meredith® Books are dedicated to providing you with information and ideas to enhance your home.
We welcome your comments and suggestions. Write to us at:
Meredith Books Editorial Department, 1716 Locust St.,
Des Moines, IA 50309-3023.
*Celebrate the Season* is available by mail.
To order editions from past years, call 800/627-5490.

If you would like to purchase any of our cooking, home decorating and design, crafts, gardening, or home improvement books,
check wherever quality books are sold. Or visit us at: bhgbooks.com.
Cover Photograph: Jay Wilde

Our seal assures you every recipe in Celebrate the Season 2005 has been tested in the Better Homes and Gardens® Test Kitchen. This means that each recipe is practical and reliable, and meets our high standards of taste appeal. We guarantee your satisfaction with this book for as long as you own it.

# the times

they are a'changing, or so the song and saying lead us to believe. But are they changing or simply cycling back to simpler days? "Handmade" and "home cooked" are once again adjectives that carry a sense of value. The home is becoming more and more of a sanctuary against the busy, impersonal world. A night out is more likely to be a gathering at someone's home than a tour of the town. Check out the wine-tasting party on pages 94–103 for a celebration that's both elegant and easy. You'll find tips on serving wines and great recipes and craft ideas that give the party a sophisticated edge. The elaborate cakes on pages 86–93 are the perfect way to make a holiday meal memorable. Peek into the home of an avid collector (pages 26–31) to see how vintage ornaments fill rooms with updated takes on nostalgic trimmings. Throughout the rest of the book, you'll find decorating ideas, gifts for both adults and kids, and seasonal items such as package wraps, ornaments, and wreaths that remind you that quite often, change is good.

*Jilann Severson*

Jilann Severson

## Ornamental Display

■ Show off your display of vintage or handmade ornaments in an unusual way. Instead of having them blend in with others on the tree, build a special box with compartments that show each ornament to its best advantage. Lay the ornaments out on paper and draw your pattern around them, then build a wooden box to fit the pattern.

# table *of* contents

## setting the stage

Spread the spirit of the season throughout your home from fall through all of winter with lamps, luminaries, table settings, wreaths, trees, ornaments, and other trims that offer up a feeling of warmth and welcome.

## gathering together

'Tis the season for reuniting with family and friends. Celebrate in style with tablesettings and recipes that range from lighthearted to sophisticated. A wine-tasting party offers up a fun way to try something new and get guests mingling.

## giving from the heart

Gifts have a special meaning when they come from the hands as well as the heart. These items, ranging from the personal to the functional, all have that "made just for you" feel that show you care.

## just for kids

The young as well as the young at heart will love the whimsical designs and bright colors that fill these pages. Make them for—or with—your favorite kids.

5

Let brightness and

# SETTING the STAGE

7

**cheer abound** as the holidays draw near this year. Accents made from fall's finest bounty, trees ranging from traditional to contemporary, clever package wraps, wreaths that sparkle, stockings that make you smile, handmade ornaments packed with color, and quick little touches all come together quickly to fill these pages as well as your home.

# absolutely gourd-eous!

**Bins at farmer's markets** and roadside stands overflow with gourds of all sizes and shapes every fall. Pay special attention to the graceful shapes of some of the plainer varieties. They're often the most dramatic when dried, painted, and stained.

## little luminaries

Autumnal stars twinkle when votive cups are placed inside gourds dotted with woodburned holes. Be sure to select gourds large enough to accommodate straight-sided votive cups that are at least 2½ inches tall.

1 Dry and prepare the gourds as described on *page 11*.

2 Using the crafts knife and the technique described on *page 12*, cut a 3-inch round hole in the bottom of each gourd. Make sure the gourds sit flat. If necessary, slightly shave the bottoms of the gourds so they sit flat.

3 Clean out the plant material.

4 Working in a well-ventilated room or outdoors, use the woodburning tool to burn a circle through the gourd. Burn two more holes to create the three-dot triangular motif. See the photograph *right* for details.

5 Repeat the burning process around the entire gourd, placing the motifs about 2 inches apart.

6 Paint the gourd with a light coat of raw umber watercolor. Use the brown marker to make stripes on the stems. After the paint dries, spray the gourds with varnish.

7 Place a tea light in a votive cup and slip the gourd over the cup. Make sure the candle's wick is trimmed short so the flame does not touch the gourd. Never leave burning candles unattended or use a candle without the cup.

### What You'll Need...

- Dried gourds with stems attached
- Crafts knife
- Straight-sided votive cups
- Woodburning tool with a ¼-inch-diameter round tip
- Raw umber watercolor
- Paintbrush
- Brown marker
- Water-based spray varnish
- Tea light candles

## What You'll Need...

- [ ] Large round gourd that sits level (the one shown is approximately 9 inches in diameter)
- [ ] Pencil
- [ ] Crafts knife
- [ ] Black acrylic paint and raw umber watercolor
- [ ] Paintbrushes
- [ ] Water-based spray varnish
- [ ] 2-inch-wide aluminum tape (available at hardware stores)
- [ ] 1¾-inch-diameter circular drinking glass, bottle, or cardboard template
- [ ] Scissors
- [ ] Spoon
- [ ] 5 feet of 16- to 18-gauge black wire
- [ ] Drill with bit slightly larger than the wire diameter
- [ ] ½- to ¾-inch-diameter twig cut the same length as the diameter of the basket
- [ ] 4 black pony beads
- [ ] Needlenose pliers

# in the round

∾ Dots of shiny aluminum tape combine with a gourd and a twig for a basket that boasts an intriguing mix of rustic and elegant elements. Use gourds of any size, adjusting the size of the dots to keep it all in scale.

1 Dry and prepare the gourd as described *right*.

2 Determine the placement of the top of the basket. It should be above the halfway point so the basket curves in slightly. Mark the top line with a pencil and cut along the line using the technique described on *page 12*.

3 Clean out the gourd. Paint the inside black and the outside with a light coat of raw umber. After the paint dries, spray the basket with varnish.

4 On the backside of the tape, trace 15 to 20 circles, 1¾ inches in diameter. Cut out the circles.

5 Peel the backing off the tape and adhere the circles in a random pattern. Let some circles overlap the top, trimming them even with the upper edge. Using the back of a spoon, gently burnish the circles onto the gourd. The circles may have slight wrinkles due to the curve of the basket and will become shinier as they are burnished.

6 Drill a hole through one end of the twig, placing the hole 1 inch from the twig's end. Drill a matching hole at the other end of the twig. Cut the wire in half. Thread one section of wire through each hole, centering the wire. Twist the wire on the underside of the handle to secure it.

7 Drill two holes, 1 inch apart, halfway up the basket. Drill matching holes directly opposite the first set.

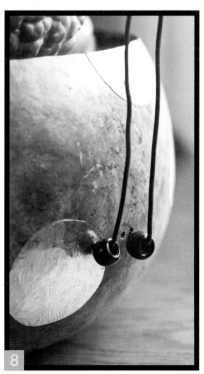

8

Determine the desired length of the wire and add 2 inches. Cut the wire to this length. Slide a pony bead onto each wire. Bend the wires back 90 degrees, placing the bend 2 inches from the ends. Slide the wires through the corresponding holes in the gourd. See the photograph *below left* for details.

9 Working on the inside of the basket, very carefully bend the wire tails upward. Use caution to avoid cracking or splitting the fragile gourd.

## *preparing gourds*

■ To dry gourds, place freshly picked gourds in a warm, dry place that has good air circulation. Make sure the gourds are firm and free of blemishes before purchasing and drying them. Always purchase extra gourds as it is common for 25 percent or more of the gourds to mold during drying. Check and turn the gourds every week. Drying may take anywhere from a few weeks to several months depending on the size and moisture content of the gourd and the humidity and warmth of your drying area.

■ Once the gourds are dry they will have a paper-like skin that needs to be removed. Soak the gourds in warm water and keep them damp while working at this stage. Using a paring knife or crafts knife, gently scrape the skin from the gourd. Let the gourd dry thoroughly before painting, drawing, or cutting.

11

## What You'll Need...

- Flat, round gourd, about 6 to 8 inches in diameter
- Crafts knife
- Chinese white and raw umber watercolor paint (optional)
- Paintbrush (optional)
- Pencil with eraser
- Ultrafine black permanent marker
- Ice pick, stylus, or awl
- Water-based spray varnish
- Lamp assembly kit (available at hardware, home improvement, and lamp repair stores)
- Purchased wooden base for vases or lamps (available at crafts stores)
- Clip-style lampshade
- Black jumbo rickrack
- Hot-glue gun and low-temp glue sticks
- Black wool felt
- White shirt buttons in assorted sizes

# lighten up

A petite gourd fashions the base of an accent lamp. Dainty scrollwork and a button-trimmed chandelier shade give it artistic appeal.

1 Dry and prepare the gourd as described on *page 11*.

2 Using the technique described *right*, cut a 1-inch hole in the top and a slightly larger hole in the bottom. Clean out all the plant material. Make sure the gourd sits flat. If necessary, slightly shave the bottom of the gourd so it sits flat.

3 For dark gourds, mix Chinese white and raw umber watercolor paints and paint the gourd. Let it dry completely. Light-colored gourds do not need paint. Using a pencil, draw the swirls on the lamp using the pattern on *page 157* as a guide. Adjust the swirls to fit your gourd. Draw some swirls from the top down and some from the bottom up. Start with the large line shown in black. Add the small branches shown in blue. Finish with the "antennae" shown in red. End each line with a small dot. Rework the design and erase any lines until the design is satisfactory to you.

4 Trace over the lines with the ultrafine marker. Using a sharp tool, make a small hole over each dot. Spray the gourd with varnish.

## cutting gourds

To make cutting the gourds easier and help prevent cracking and breaking, draw the cutting line with a pencil. Using a crafts knife, puncture small slits along the pencil line so it resembles a dotted line. Use the knife to cut between the lines. Smooth out any uneven spots.

5 Assemble the lamp according to the kit. See the photograph *above* for details. Use a cap to cover the top hole and place the wooden base at the bottom. Threaded pipe keeps the lamp stable. If necessary, use an adapter to fit the bulb to the socket.

6 For the shade, glue rickrack to the bottom so half the trim extends beyond the lower edge of the shade. Cut the felt into ½-inch-wide strips. Glue the strips over the top of the rickrack to form a straight upper line. Glue additional strips around the top of the shade. On the bottom edge, glue buttons to the felt strip, placing a button directly over the curve of the lower rickrack edge.

12

# fall welcomes

The coming of autumn brings with it a frenzy of colors not seen at any other time. Some hues become richer and more subtle while others take on a lush brilliance.

## unexpected beauty

❧ Grace an entryway with atypical fall beauties. Brilliant green hedge apples and russet berries piled in a rusted urn form an unusual topiary. On the door, a cornucopia made of window screen holds dried hydrangea blooms and leaves.

### HEDGE APPLE TOPIARY

1 Fit the cone into the urn and secure it with florist's tape. The cone should be about equal in height to the urn. If it is too tall, cut off the top point.

2 Starting at the bottom of the urn, attach the hedge apples to the cone with toothpicks and skewers. It may take several picks to hold each in place and you may need to also attach them to each other. If necessary, further secure them with hot glue.

3 Fill in the spaces with berry sprigs, trimming them as necessary.

4 Replace the hedge apples as needed; they may decay over time.

### What You'll Need...

- ☐ Urn or other container
- ☐ Plastic foam cone to fit the container
- ☐ Florist's tape
- ☐ Hedge apples
- ☐ Toothpicks and thin wooden skewers
- ☐ Fall berry picks and sprigs
- ☐ Wire cutters or scissors
- ☐ Hot-glue gun and low-temperature glue sticks

### SCREEN CORNUCOPIA

1 Cut the screen into a 24-inch circle. Cut from the outer edge to the middle. NOTE: To prevent injury, wear work gloves and a long-sleeve shirt when working with screen.

2 Roll the screen into a cone shape, trimming as necessary. Open the cone and encase the raw edges with tape. (First aid tape works well.) Paint both sides of the screen rust color.

3 Shape the screen into the cornucopia. Overlap the edges and secure them with small pieces of fine wire.

4 Paint the leaves gold and glue them to the upper edge of the cornucopia. Attach the bead or charm to the tip with fine wire.

5 Using pliers, shape one end of the copper wire into a small loop to hold the cornucopia tip. Spiral the remaining wire into large flat concentric circles around the loop. Leave the last 8 inches straight.

6 Open the circles to hold the cone. Shape the straight end into a hanging spiral. Add dried hydrangeas or other fall flowers.

15

## What You'll Need...

- [ ] 2 feet of window screen
- [ ] Tin snips
- [ ] ½-inch-wide fabric tape
- [ ] Gold and rust spray paint
- [ ] Fine-gauge florist's wire
- [ ] Small silk leaves
- [ ] Hot-glue gun and low-temperature glue sticks
- [ ] Large bead or charm
- [ ] 6-gauge copper wire
- [ ] Needlenose pliers

16

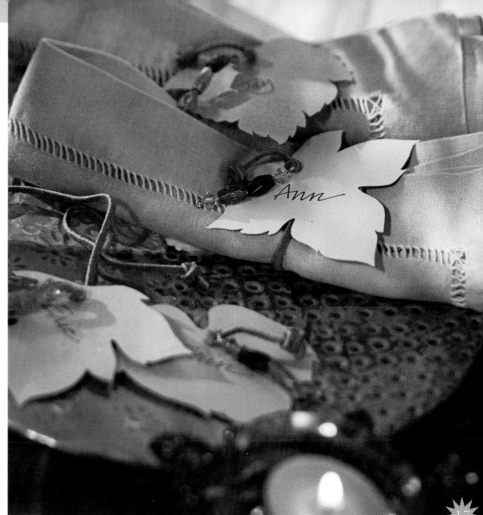

# leafy tableau

❧ Bring the feel of fall to your table by using one of the standard fall motifs—leaves—as overlays on a purchased table runner and for matching napkin rings.

### TABLE RUNNER LEAVES

**1** Enlarge the leaf patterns on *page 156* to fit both the width of your runner and the length of your table.

**2** Cut the leaves from wool felt, alternating the colors.

**3** Pin contrasting ribbon along the edges of leaf shapes. Sew down the center of the ribbon using matching thread. Place the leaves over the table runner at even intervals.

### LEAF NAPKIN TIES

**1** Enlarge the leaf patterns on *page 156* to scale. Cut the shapes from card stock.

**2** Thread the beads onto the head pins, creating 2-inch bead strands. Loop the end of each head pin.

**3** Cut the leather cord into 10-inch-long strips. Run one end through the loops of the bead strands and tie a half-knot.

**3** Punch a hole in the leaf and set the eyelet. Thread the leaf onto the cord and knot it in place. Knot the remaining end.

**4** Loosely tie the cords around napkins.

## What You'll Need...

**FOR TABLE RUNNER LEAVES:**
- [ ] Wool felt in fall colors to match your table runner
- [ ] 3/16-inch contrasting organdy ribbon
- [ ] Thread to match

**FOR LEAF NAPKIN TIES:**
- [ ] Card stock in assorted fall colors
- [ ] Assorted beads
- [ ] 3-inch head pin
- [ ] Leather cord
- [ ] Hole punch and matching eyelets to fit the leather cord

▶ Line Lights: Add dots of light down a buffet or dining table with colorful votive lights. Line an antique bread tray with votive cups and tea lights, making sure they sit flat. A flat weathered or color-washed board can be substituted for the bread board. Never leave burning candles unattended and keep all items away from the flames.

# In a Twinkling:
# fall into it...

◀ Coasting Along: Set your table in style with fall-themed coasters. Decoupage plain ceramic tiles with torn bits of tissue paper. Add ribbon borders, wrapping and gluing the ends to the back of the tile. Finish it all with fall stickers and several coats of acrylic glaze. Add a felt backing to prevent scratching any surfaces.

Tiny Treasures: Turn miniature gourds into an elegant centerpiece by adding rickrack, pearls, or other trims. Line the gourds with assorted trims or spiral the decorations around the gourd. Use sequin pins to hold it all in place.

▲ Fall Wraps: Make fall packages as pretty as the scenes outdoors with silk leaf embellishments. Trim glittered leaves from their stems and glue them to boxes or bags. Add beads, berries, and ribbons for trims.

▲ Call It Mellow Yellow: Cast a golden glow with votive cups covered in yellow tissue paper. Tear tissue paper into small pieces, then decoupage it to the surface of plain, straight-sided votive cups. Add fall stickers and top it all with a layer of acrylic glaze. Use tea lights in the votive cups to keep the flames low. Never leave burning candles unattended.

# connect the dots

Sprinkle your home with dotty charm this season. Cheery polka dots hit the spot as they lighten and brighten everyone's mood.

## jester trim

◔ Butcher paper is transformed into shelf trim when folded and cut paper-doll style. Use a paper punch to make the upper holes, and dot stickers to add circles to the ends.

## table in the round

◔ You'll be seeing spots at this perky table, *opposite*. Even the dinnerware takes on the look of polka dots when different colors are layered together. Spotty napkins and place mats look festive during the holidays but could be used year round. A scattering of oranges makes for the simplest of centerpieces and adds even more dots of color.

## squiggles and dots

◔ Painted wooden balls wound with spiraled chenille strips pack the punchy tree in the background. To make the ornaments, cut chenille strips in half. Twist two strips to fit around a 1-inch wooden ball, but do not place them on the ball. Attach six more strips to the center ring and coil the ends to resemble spirals. Slip the ball into the chenille strip trim and hot-glue it in place.

21

# spotty, dotty place mats

Round up some fun with circular place mats. For each place mat, cut two 18-inch circles of contrasting fabrics. Baste a matching circle of batting to the wrong side of one fabric circle. With right sides facing, sew the circles together leaving an opening for turning. Turn, press, and slip-stitch the opening closed. Starting at the outside edge and working inward, machine-quilt the place mat in concentric circles, spacing the stitched rows ¼ inch apart. Leave the center 4½ inches unquilted.

# seeing spots

ﮩ Whether it's Happy Holi*dots* or Happy Holi*days,* this greeting makes anyone smile. Cut letters from card stock or use die-cut letters. Spray the fronts of the letters and the back of dotted papers with spray glue. Press them together and trim away the excess paper. Add eyelets on each side of each letter and string the banner together with ribbon.

# a dotting of trees

ﮩ This forest of polka-dot fabric trees looks like the ornaments were already hung in place. To make the trees, pin quilt batting over a variety of sizes of plastic foam cones. NOTE: Snip off the tip of the cone to make it easier to attach the fabric and the ball topper. Trim away the excess batting. Tightly wrap the trees in fabric, turning under the raw edges and trimming away any excess fabric. Pin or slip-stitch the fabric over the cones. Paint flat-sided wooden balls (often called doll's heads) in contrasting colors. Glue one ball to the base and one to the top.

23

# dots of light

ﮩ A blizzard of dots turns plain glass hurricanes into upbeat beacons of holiday spirit. Press round stickers from office supply stores to the hurricanes, then put a pillar candle inside the glass. After the holidays, the stickers peel right off.

## crystal lights

❧ Glass garlands take on a rich glow when illuminated by white lights, adding a magical touch to a wreath. Wrap the wreath form with the lights so the plug falls at the top and the cord can be concealed by the ribbon. Wire the lights in place so they are spaced evenly. Wrap the garlands over the wreath in serpentine fashion, covering the entire wreath form and hiding as many lights as possible. Wire the garlands in place. (If necessary, use needlenose pliers or similar tools to coax the garlands in place.) Loop the hanging ribbon through the top of the wreath form so it covers the light cord. Wire dowels to the ribbon's stress point and the back of the wreath. Finish with additional ribbon bows.

### What You'll Need...

- ☐ 12-inch-diameter wire wreath form
- ☐ 120 white miniature lights with a white cord
- ☐ Garlands: pink glass, green glass, and pearl bead cluster
- ☐ Needlenose pliers
- ☐ 1 yard 3-inch-wide ribbons in matching colors
- ☐ Three 3x¼-inch dowels
- ☐ 30-gauge silver florist's wire

## flurry of fun

❧ Feathers, snowflakes, and snowballs mix it up for an indoor blizzard that can last the whole winter season. Using U-shape florist's pins, cover the wreath form with the feather boa. Spray the plastic foam balls with artificial snow so they resemble snowballs. For interest, vary the size of the balls. Hot-glue the snowballs to the wreath. Cut some of the snowflakes in half and tuck them into the wreath form so they radiate in different directions. Wire the remaining

# wreaths without

## What You'll Need...

- U-shape florist's pins
- 21-inch-diameter white plastic foam wreath form
- White feather boa
- Plastic foam balls
- Spray snow
- Hot-glue gun and low-temperature glue sticks
- White and silver snowflake ornaments
- Silver florist's wire
- Blue satin ribbon

snowflakes flat to the wreath. Cut the ribbon into pieces and shape the pieces into loops and loose bows. Wire the ribbons to the wreath, tucking them around the snowflakes and snowballs.

# silver exchange

❧ Trade in traditional greens for a mass of silver balls. Start with a round mirror surrounded by a square frame. The one shown *above* measures 21 inches square. Pound several nails into each outside corner. Wrap the wire around the broomstick to make loops. Attach the looped wire to the nails so the wire encircles the frame several times. Gather the ornaments into clusters and twist their wires together. Wire the clusters to the looped wire until the frame is covered but the

## What You'll Need...

- Round mirror with a square silver frame
- Small nails
- 10-gauge wire
- Broomstick or dowel
- Silver ornaments with wire stems
- Silver florist's wire
- Crystals and prisms

mirror is still visible. For interest, mix matte and shiny balls and vary the sizes. Some of the looped wire may remain visible. Using silver-colored florist's wire, attach crystals and prisms so they dangle from the wreath.

# greens
## Add an elegant welcome to your home with wreaths that sparkle and shine.

Infuse glitter, glamour, and a little history into holiday décor with antique ornaments from this century and last.

# vintage vignettes

It was a search through flea market treasures and trash that got antiques collector Jo Brantley of Carlisle, Iowa, started collecting vintage ornaments more than 20 years ago. She spotted some old ornaments and liked their color and patina. She bought them. Then she bought more. Before she knew it, she had an antique ornament collection large enough to cover a small tree. As her collection grew to over 2,000 ornaments, so too did the size of her tree.

From ornaments that graced 19th-century holiday trees in Europe to more "modern" American ones from the 1940s and 1950s, Jo hangs them all with equanimity. "I just love the old ornaments," she says. "You wonder what all the stories are." Christmas has always been her favorite holiday. "At Christmas, the child in me comes out, and the ornaments fulfill that dream." Her favorite ornament? The one that her mother gave her; it hung on their family tree when Jo was a little girl.

Made from the thinnest of glass, vintage ornaments are fragile and require careful handling when hanging, taking down, and storing. Jo protects her collection by placing it in wooden trunks. She layers the trunk with a cushion of tissue and makes sure the ornaments don't touch. Some collectors individually wrap ornaments using old dress patterns or tissue paper, or store them in containers specially made for protecting fragile items.

Jo's antique ornament collection has immigrated from her Christmas tree to unexpected places all over her house, spreading its timeless holiday beauty. The wreath shown *above* is testimony to Jo's creative way with display. A silk wreath wired with ornaments is held to a window with suction cups. Jo then perched an old frame around the wreath and added the holiday greeting.

## layered luxury

ᘯ Most of Jo's ornament collection cloaks her holiday tree in history and color. Santas and dancing bears, teardrops and orbs, hand-painted and gemlike glass— Jo liberally heaps antique ornaments onto her tree with care and artistry. Intricate and unusual ornaments include those dressed up with an overlay of twisted wire or scenes painted with glitter. As a finishing touch, Jo drapes the tree with garlands of her collection of vintage pearl necklaces, also foraged from flea markets and yard sales.

## candy-colored splendor

ᘯ A footed apothecary jar shows off the charms of jewel-toned glass vintage ornaments. This crystal clear vessel allows even the smallest of ornaments to shine. With light from a nearby window, the prism-effect creates a kaleidoscope of candy color throughout the room. Table ornaments nested on ornate doorknob backs carry the twinkle and magic beyond the jar.

29

# candelabra chic

✍ Candelabras lend elegance to any table, but exchanging flame-shaped tree toppers for candles creates an unexpected centerpiece—and a perfect way to display a unique collection. The narrow bases of antique (and new) tree toppers make them ideal for candleholder display. The perfect accessory to top off this sophisticated candelabra? A string of pearls and diamond-like cut-glass beads, of course.

# a garden of glitter

✍ A lineup of new and antique ornaments creates a garden of glitter on this mantelpiece corner. Seated in single candleholders and held in place with floral clay, multitiered tree toppers take on the illusion of elegantly bedecked topiary trees. Among them, a bouquet of vintage glass-beaded florist's sticks blossoms from a ribbed, clear-glass vase. Miniature topiary-shaped ornaments support the theme.

# what a kick!

## Give plain old stockings the boot this year, replacing them with painted canvas boot shapes.

## painted canvas boots and skirt

### What You'll Need...

- [ ] 2½ yards of 60-inch-wide #10 cotton canvas
- [ ] Towel or press cloth
- [ ] Hard lead pencil
- [ ] #14 round artist's brush
- [ ] Plaid Folk Art acrylic paint: Pure Gold, Christmas Red, Poppy Red, Yellow Citron, Pure Orange, School Bus Yellow, Light Fuchsia, Kelly Green, Green
- [ ] Hot-glue gun and low-temp glue sticks
- [ ] Cording for hanging
- [ ] Pushpin
- [ ] String

Artist's canvas takes on a new purpose when sewn into boot shapes and painted with lively colors. The no-sew tree skirt is packed with painted presents so you'll have gifts under the tree long before Santa arrives.

**1** Enlarge the patterns on *page 157* to scale. Cut a front and a back for each stocking shape, adding ¼-inch seams.

**2** With right sides facing, sew the stocking front to the back, leaving the top edge open. For the pointed stocking *below right*, sew only to the fold line, then clip from the seam allowance to the stitching line at the fold. For the other stockings, sew to the top. Turn the stocking right side out. For the pointed stocking, sew from the fold line to the end of the outer points. Right sides of the fabric will still be facing but the seam allowance will be exposed. Fold the stocking down over itself along the fold line, forming the cuff.

**3** Cover the stocking with a towel or press cloth and iron it to flatten down all the seams.

**4** Trace the cuff and tab onto the canvas. Paint a gold line over the pencil line. Cut out the pieces.

**5** For the cuffed stocking *below center*, sew the short ends of the cuff together with right sides facing. Slip the cuff into the stocking so the upper edges align and the right side of the cuff faces the wrong side of the stocking. Sew around the upper edge. Turn and press the cuff to the right side, encasing the seam.

**6** Paint the stockings and cuffs in geometric or whimsical patterns. See the stockings *left* for design ideas. For the cowboy boot stocking *far left*, glue the tabs in place. Tack cord loops to the upper corner of each stocking for hanging.

**7** For the tree skirt, fold a 50-inch square of canvas in quarters. Place a pushpin at the corner fold. Tie one end of a piece of string to the pushpin and the other to a pencil, leaving 24 inches between the pin and the pencil. Draw an arc from edge to edge. Repeat using 6 inches of string. Cut along both lines. Open the canvas and cut from the outside edge to the inside circle. Paint the wrong side along all the cut edges to prevent them from fraying.

**8** Paint box shapes onto the skirt. See the photograph *above* for design ideas. Paint the edges gold. Paint concentric circles between the boxes.

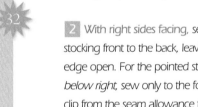

32

# pretty in pink

Be a softie this season by filling your home with gentle pinks and plenty of white. Old-fashioned ornaments add to the relaxing feel of a home packed with lighthearted colors.

## rosy wreaths

❧ A free-form wire ornament with the look of wild grapevine mixes the best of the rustic and the refined. Wrap a 6-foot length of 16-gauge annealed wire into an uneven circle. Wrap the ends around a pencil to form tendrils. Interweave two more lengths of wire so they are unevenly shaped. Wash and dry the wire thoroughly, then spray-paint it white. Wire silk and velvet flowers to the bottom third of the wreath and leave the remaining portion of the wreath open.

## color me pink

❧ Pink papers and ribbons in mix and match patterns are trimmed in the most elaborate ways. Cut-outs of Victorian figurines, silk flowers, and miniature ornaments make the packages almost too pretty to open. By using the same elements on the packages as are used on the tree, the room comes together with a strong, unified look.

## memory tree

❧ Old-fashioned ornaments pack a tree with charm—and memories. Intricate cut-paper snowflakes and paper Victorian figurines get a bit of a perk from a bright cranberry garland. Purchase similar figurine cut-outs and hang them on the tree or make your own from clip art, adding glitter paint for a bit of sparkle.

## the up and up

❧ Turn an ornament upside down by sitting it on a branch of a sparse feather tree rather than dangling it downward. Hot-glue miniature ornaments into reproduction clip-style candle holders, then attach them to the branches so the balls face up.

## in the pink

❧ Twin white feather trees become the room's focal point during the holidays, but like fraternal twins each has its own distinct look. One is sparsely decorated with just a few retro ornaments and the other drips with sparkle and a cedar garland. But both reflect the room's pink palette and its nod to vintage and Victorian collectibles.

# it's in the details...

❧ The details tucked here and there give the room the finishing touches that make it look like a lived-in showroom. *Clockwise from upper left:* URNING APPROVAL: A small whitewashed metal urn finds a winter home on the mantel, surrounded by greenery and silk flowers and piled high with ornaments. FLOWERS ON ICE: Paperwhite narcissus forced in acrylic ice chips instead of the traditional river rocks give the arrangement a fresh, sparkling look. There's no need for soil; simply nestle the bulbs in the ice chips, add water, and let them sprout. BACK TO THE FUTURE: Plastic ornaments from the 1950s are part snowflake, part starburst, and a little bit Sputnik, making them work well in an eclectic setting.

# dancing stars

∾ Add twinkle to your window with aluminum stars. The valance shown here hangs from a branch for contrast, but a purchased rod works just as well.

1 Enlarge the star patterns on *page* 157 to size and cut five of each size from aluminum flashing. Cut the points blunt and hammer the edges smooth. Drill a small hole in each star.

2 Drill a hole through the branch at its center. Evenly space two holes on either side of the center hole. Thread 30 inches of monofilament through each hole and knot it at the top. Trim the monofilament strands to 19 inches.

3 Thread a star of each size onto the monofilament. Arrange them as desired and secure them using small pieces of aluminum tape adhered to their backs.

4 For the branch's hanging loops, cut the ribbon to the desired length plus 3 inches. Thread the ribbon through the rings. Turn under the raw edges of the ribbon and glue them in place. Wrap the ribbon loop around the branch, allowing the top edge to overlap 2 inches at the front. See the photograph *left* for details. Glue a button to the overlap.

5 Place nails in the wall and slide the hanger rings over the nails. Hot-glue buttons over the nailheads. Slip the branch into the hanging loops.

# over the top

Bring holiday cheer to your windows with festive valances made from dancing stars or dangling teacups.

## What You'll Need...

- ☐ Aluminum flashing
- ☐ Tin snips
- ☐ Hammer and fine-grit sandpaper (optional)
- ☐ Drill with a small bit
- ☐ Tree branch about 1 inch thick and slightly longer than the window width
- ☐ Monofilament
- ☐ Aluminum tape
- ☐ Ribbon for hanging loops
- ☐ 2 small drapery rings
- ☐ 4 vintage buttons
- ☐ 2 flat-head nails

# teatime

🍂 Vintage teacups and miniature teapots lend a playful look to a holiday tea party. These feature seasonal red and green but other colors could hang around all year.

**1** Knot the end of a ribbon to the handle of each teacup. Trim the tail to ½ inch; hot-glue the tail to the ribbon.

**2** Cut the ribbons to the desired length plus 3 inches. Loop the end of the ribbon to the wrong side and hot-glue the layers together, leaving an opening to insert the rod.

**3** Slide the ribbons over the rod and hang the rod, adjusting the cups and finials as needed. Make bows from the ribbon scraps and hot-glue them to the teacup handles to cover the knots.

**4** Using industrial-strength glue, join the teapot lids to the teapots. When dry, glue the bases of the teapots to the end caps of the rod. See the photograph *above left* for details. Let dry.

**5** To make matching tiebacks, glue saucers to plain tieback hardware using industrial-strength glue. See the photograph *right* for details.

## What You'll Need...

- [ ] 1 yard red or green ribbon for each teacup
- [ ] Assorted teacups in red and green patterns
- [ ] Hot-glue gun and low-temp glue sticks
- [ ] Curtain rod with vinyl end caps
- [ ] Industrial-strength glue
- [ ] Miniature teapots
- [ ] Curtain rod hardware
- [ ] Curtain tieback (optional)
- [ ] Red and green saucers (optional)

39

◀ Simple Greeting: Tuck a tiny greeting anywhere this season. Center adhesive scrapbooking letters on small candles, then arrange the candles to spell out your favorite message. Never leave burning candles unattended.

# In a Twinkling:
# decorations

◀ Fire and Ice: Cylinders of ice and white pillar candles offer up an unusual welcome for cold-weather festivities. Freeze water in plastic cylindrical vases of various sizes (available at floral supply stores), then fill an urn, birdbath, or other shallow outdoor container with snow. Run the vases under water to remove the ice cylinders and arrange them and some candles in the snow.

▶ Packaged Goods: A brightly colored gift-box topiary offers a fun variation to the traditional boxwood or ivy variety of sculpted shapes. Wrap graduated boxes in bright papers, then hot-glue them into a stack. Prop them on top of a planter that is slightly smaller in diameter than the largest box. If desired, hot-glue the bottom box to the rim of the planter to keep the arrangement secure.

◀ Tabletop Display: A two-level centerpiece custom-made from flea market finds is a prefect fit for this Santa display. Remove the legs from a small and a larger end table, saving one leg for the tier between the two levels. Assemble the platforms with glue and screws, add ball feet, and paint the entire piece white. If flea markets or garage sales don't yield the proper makings, similar materials can be found at crafts and home improvement stores.

41

◀ A Light Touch: Dress a lampshade for the holidays with bright baubles and fluffy ribbon. Glue or tack ribbon to the bottom edge of the shade, then stitch little ornaments to the lower edge. After the holidays, remove the trims or simply store the shade until next year and replace it with a plain one.

# wrap artistry

From the drawing diva to the artistically impaired, everyone can make custom gift wraps, cards, and tags using a home computer, cut papers, rubber stamps, or even crayons.

## thumb-thing special

A green thumb is all it takes to grow these polka-dot trees. Spread a small amount of green paint onto a paper plate. Dip your thumb lightly into the paint, then gently press it onto the paper and repeat, creating a polka-dot pattern. After the paint dries, use paint pens and glitter glue to decorate the trees and add trunks and stars.

For the card, make a row of trees across the front of folded card stock.

To create the tag, stamp a single tree on a small white label. Place the label on green card stock and trim it to size.

## bubble up

This flurry of snowballs is created in the most clever of ways. Brush white acrylic paint over the textured side of ordinary bubble wrap, then press the paint onto plain blue paper. Use an even pressure, then peel away the bubble wrap.

For the card, stamp and emboss a snowflake onto card stock. Layer paper of other colors and a scrap of the blue dot paper below the embossed design and glue them together.

To create the tag, do a miniature version of the card, layering the papers as desired.

# warm wishes

Rows of patterned mittens hang from a hand-drawn clothesline to give plain red paper a bold graphic look. Draw a mitten shape onto thick white paper for a template, then cut it out. Using the template, cut mittens from scraps of gift wrap or scrapbooking papers. Draw clotheslines across the paper. Glue the mittens to the clotheslines as if they were hanging. Add brown rectangles for clothespins.

For the card, glue a mitten to the front of folded card stock, adding a clothespin if desired.

For the tag, glue gift wrap to two pieces of card stock. Cut out mitten shapes in the desired size. Punch a hole in the center of each mitten and join the two with ribbon or string.

# shades of yesterday

Turn a cherished photograph into memorable gift wrap by reproducing the image on a computer or photocopier.

Make a single copy of the photograph (enlarge and crop it as desired). To use a computer, scan the cropped image and repeat it in rows across the paper. To use a photocopier, make multiple copies, tape them together, and make one final copy of the full sheet.

For the card, glue a single image to blank card stock. Frame it with tinsel glued over the edges. Print or hand-letter a greeting onto contrasting paper. Cut out the greeting with decorative scissors and glue it to the card.

To create the tag, reduce the size of the photo and print it onto a sticker or copy it onto plain paper and cut it out. Adhere the photo to a purchased tag.

Merry Christmas

# starring role

✎ Rubber stamps and foil stickers add pizzazz to plain white paper. NOTE: Use only matte-finish paper such as butcher paper, kraft paper, or matte gift wrap; stamping will smudge on non-matte paper. Randomly stamp red and green stars onto the paper. Add a foil sticker to the center of each star.

For the card, print or letter a greeting onto green card stock. Stamp a red star in the center and top it with a foil sticker.

To create the tag, stamp a red star onto white card stock. Cut around the edges with decorative-edge scissors. Stamp another star to the back of green card stock, then cut it out with straight scissors so it is slightly smaller than the stamped star. With the plain side up, glue the green star over the red star. Add a foil sticker to the center of the tag and glitter dots to the points of the star.

45

# present tense

✎ Rows of hand-drawn gift boxes capture the childlike anticipation of opening packages. Self-adhesive paper and corrugated papers make up the matching card and tag. Using crayons, draw packages of different sizes and shapes across plain white paper.

For the card, print or letter a greeting onto card stock and trim around it with decorative-edge scissors. Cut self-adhesive paper slightly larger than the greeting and adhere it to the front of card stock. Glue the greeting over the self-adhesive paper. Cut more self-adhesive paper into squares and rectangles for packages.

Cut narrow ribbons from contrasting self-adhesive paper. Adhere the packages to the card stock and top them with ribbon strips. For bows, punch flower shapes from self-adhesive paper and cut the flowers in half.

To create the tag, cut a square of corrugated paper. Glue a ribbon up the center, form a hanging loop at the top, and glue the ends to the back. Knot a ribbon scrap and glue it to the square for a bow. Write or print the recipient's name on a card stock scrap and glue it in place.

# have a ball

Color it fun this year: Make hand-painted or dipped ornaments in your favorite hues.

## What You'll Need...

- [ ] Clear glass ornaments
- [ ] Cotton balls
- [ ] Glass surface conditioner
- [ ] Newspapers
- [ ] String
- [ ] Glass paint and clear gloss glass glaze
- [ ] Custard cups
- [ ] Fine florist's wire or ornament hangers
- [ ] Gold accent liner pen for drawing on glass

## little dippers

❧ Inexpensive clear glass ornaments become works of art when dipped into one or more translucent glass glazes and encircled with gold lines.

**1** Using a cotton ball, wipe the ornament with surface conditioner. While the ball dries, prepare a work surface by lining it with a thick pad of newspaper. Hang a string clothesline over the paper for a drying area.

**2** Pour the paint into custard cups, mixing the colors if necessary to achieve the desired palette. Add glaze to make the paint the desired transparency.

Using wire or an ornament hook, hang the ornament on the string until the paint dries completely. NOTE: Paint will continue to drip off the ornaments. See the photograph *above* for details.

**5** After the paint dries, dip the ornament one or more additional times to achieve the desired colors and transparency. Use different angles and colors for each dipping or use the same angle and color to intensify a single color.

**6** If desired, decorate with gold painted lines (freehand) after the paint dries completely.

Dip the lower one-third to one-half of the ornament into the paint. Hold the ornament straight or at an angle. Let the excess paint drip back into the cup. See the photograph *above* for details.

46

48

# stripe one!

Matte-finish ornaments take on a retro look when striped with paint and glitter. Look to vintage ornaments, fashions, or magazines from the 1950s for color pattern ideas. Unusual color combinations like red, white, and turquoise; royal blue, turquoise, and gold; or orange, red, and fuchsia result in a postmodern look. Varying the width of the stripes provokes even more interest.

1

Cut a piece of ribbon to the length where you want the first stripe. Tape it in place and mark the end of the ribbon. See the photograph *above* for details. Repeat the hash marks, working your way around the ball.

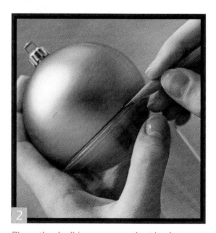

2

Place the ball in a cup so the rim is even with the hash marks. Draw your first placement line at the hash marks. See the photograph *above* for details. Place a length of tape along the line without covering the pencil mark.

3

To keep the lines parallel, use rows of narrow tape as place markers. Butt each row of tape against the previous one until the entire painting surface is covered. Remove the tape from the areas that are to be painted. See the photograph *above* for details.

4

Paint the exposed areas white. After the paint dries, paint each area with one or more coats of the desired color. See the photograph *above* for details. While the final coat of paint is still wet, shake glitter over the surface. When the paint is dry, remove the tape.

49

◄ Lucky Breaks: Don't cry over broken ornaments. Collect those that have been dropped or damaged and put them in a clear crock for a mosaic of sparkle and color. Let them catch the light near a window or use the crock as a centerpiece. Take care when handling the broken shards—wear gloves to prevent cuts. Freshen the collection every time another ornament breaks.

# In a Twinkling:
# ornaments

50

◄ Urning Approval: Give a garden-style urn a holiday look. Miniature metal, resin, and terra-cotta urns abound at crafts and decorating stores. Fill the bottom with florist's foam to take up some of the empty space. Pile the urn high with new, vintage, or reproduction ornaments. Tuck silk or fresh greenery around the rim and in any gaps to soften the look.

▶ Ring Around the Posies: Cover a cylindrical glass vase or hurricane with plain tree ornaments for an elegant holiday feel. Run string through caps of matching ornaments—the strand must be long enough to wrap around the vase. Tie the ends together so the ornaments face out and the caps do not show. Repeat with additional rows. For more stability, spot-glue the ornaments with hot glue. If desired, tuck snippets of ribbon between some of the balls (see photograph).

◀ Card Ornaments: Turn old cards or children's drawings into wooden ornaments. Scan and print or photocopy the card or drawing, cropping as desired. Using a crafts knife, cut thin balsa wood to size. Glue the artwork to the balsa, then add a backing of decorative paper. Paint the wood edges. Drill a hole for hanging and thread ribbon through the hole.

51

◀ Tree Ornament: Card stock cones decorated with eyelets and glitter hang out together to form a fanciful tree-shape ornament. Cut 3-, 3½-, and 4-inch circles from green card stock. Punch a hole at the center of each circle and cut a line from the edge to the hole. Wrap each circle into a cone and use eyelets to hold the shape. Trim each cone with additional eyelets and rims of glitter paint. To join the cones, string 2½ inches of beads onto a 16-inch length of cord. From the underside, pull the cord through the center of the largest cone so the beads are snug against the cone top. Fold and knot the cord into a loop that ends 5 inches above the cone. Knot the loop directly above the large cone. Run the loop through the remaining cones, knotting it directly above and below the cones to hold them in place. To finish the ornament, string the loop through a bead at the very top, then knot the loop to hold the bead in place.

Holidays find

52

**a way to bring people together** whether it's as casual as caroling or as formal as a wine-tasting party. Food and a pretty table are key to these events. Look to these pages for ways to treat your family and guests to special foods and settings.

# GATHERING *together*

53

Merry Christmas, Natalie

one tabletop

Dust off the dinnerware that's hidden in the china cabinet. With a few easy touches, one set of the basics is the perfect backdrop for all your holiday entertaining.

## red and white is always right

The room exudes jolly spirit when the table is done in crisp red and white. The table runner is inspired by Santa himself with strips of red felt topped by a band of white "fur." Wide ribbons wind around dinner plates, large ornaments with taglike greetings become place cards, and red and white striped napkins are folded into points reminiscent of busy little elves. For the centerpiece, a large bowl is filled with an assortment of red ornaments and surrounded by white pillar candles.

# three ways

# new year's glam and glitter

〰 A New Year's table is dressed to the nines for the magic hour of 12 o'clock. Elegant party hats and gold Moravian stars take center stage on a table sprinkled with shiny star-shape confetti. For an ethereal look, place an optional layer of white tulle over the tablecloth (it also keeps the confetti from shifting). For the place cards, silver mesh is gathered into a bag that holds more confetti. A ribbon ties the bag closed and has both the night's greeting and the guest's name attached. For a final touch of elegance, each place setting is surrounded by a narrow white feather boa. Tuck the boas under the rim of the dinner plate so the fluffy stuff won't get in the way of dining and toasting.

57

## extra touches

### RED AND WHITE RUNNER:

(Page 54) Cut an 18-inch strip of bright red felt and place it down the center of the table. It should be long enough to reach the edge of the tablecloth. Cut a 12-inch width of dark red felt and center it over the bright red felt. Finish with a 3-inch-wide band of artificial fur centered over the dark felt.

To wrap the dinner plates in ribbon, cut 3-inch-wide red ribbon the diameter of the plates plus 6 inches. Place one end of the ribbon under the plate at the back edge, using the plate to anchor it in place. Draw the ribbon over the plate and down the front of the table. Hold it in place with the salad plate. Trim the ends into points.

### NEW YEAR'S PARTY HATS:

(Below) Purchase plain inexpensive cone-shape party hats. Disassemble the hats so they lay flat. Spray the right side of the hats and the wrong side of decorative papers with spray adhesive, then press them together. Trim the paper to fit the hat. Reassemble the hats and secure them on the inside with tape. Using the hats shown below for inspiration, hot-glue trims such as tulle, pleated ribbon, upholstery fringe, wire-edged ribbon, chenille stems, tassels, and millinery trims to the hats

### ICY WREATH CENTERPIECE:

(Page 58) Purchase an ice-covered twig wreath. Draw small ornaments into a cluster by running the wire through the tops. Use the wire tails to attach the ornaments to the wreath.

58

# winter wonder

Whether you hail from Alaska, Alabama, or anywhere in between, winter brings thoughts of snow and ice. That same sparkling feel spreads to the table when it is done all in white. A purchased twig wreath coated with tiny acrylic ice pellets moves in as a centerpiece. New and vintage silver ornaments and sheer silver ribbon give the wreath a focal point. White candles in clear glass holders fit both inside and outside the wreath. When lit, their flames make the wreath, candlesticks, and stemware sparkle like icicles. Plain white napkins edged with loopy lace replicate freshly fallen snow; the ribbed napkin holders impart an icy feel. Computer-generated name cards sport snowflake appliques in white and silver.

60

# star light, star bright

Bring bright, contemporary flair to this year's Hanukkah celebration.

Hanukkah is the season of light, so spread that lightness to your table with sparkling Star of David symbols. Pretty enough to leave out for all eight days, the table and accessories feature a two-tone silk dupioni table scarf that's knotted at the center, beaded and glittered candle bobeches, silver confetti stars to scatter on the table, and gift bags for each family member or guest.

# knot of appeal

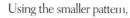 For the table runner, determine the desired length and width for your table. Allow for a loose knot at the center and drape at each end. Cut the runner on the crosswise grain from two shades of blue silk dupioni, allowing for piecing the fabrics at the center of the runner. Sew each color together along one short edge, forming a long strip.

With right sides facing, sew the darker fabric to the lighter fabric along the long edges, leaving an opening for turning. Sew across both short edges. NOTE: Due to the nature of the fabric, the two strips will probably not align perfectly. Trim away any excess fabric and clip the corners. Turn the runner right side out and slip-stitch the opening closed.

Lightly press the runner. Loosely knot it at the center to conceal the seams. Flip it so one half has the light side up and the other has the dark side up.

# twinkling stars

 For the confetti stars, spray-glue two pieces of silver card stock together with wrong sides facing. Enlarge the star pattern on *page* 157 to scale and cut stars from the card stock. Mark the taping line. Adhere ¼-inch-wide double-stick tape to the wrong side of ¼-inch-wide silver ribbon. Cut six pieces of ribbon to fit each star along the taping line, mitering the corners. Remove the tape backing and stick the ribbon to the stars.

# star treatment

Top each candlestick with a Star of David bobeche for the holiday. Dangling beads and mica snow or glitter add sparkle, especially when the candles are lit.

To make the bobeches, enlarge the pattern on *page* 157 to scale. For each bobeche, cut two large stars from poster board. Use a crafts knife to cut out the center circle. Glue the stars together with spray adhesive. Using decoupage medium, glue a square of silver metallic paper to the star, pressing it so the star edges are obvious. Slash through the paper at the center circle.

Turn back the slashed portions and glue them in place. Repeat on the other side with blue paper, cutting a circle for the hole instead of slashing it. Using pinking shears, trim the excess paper from around the star shape. At each inner point, use a needle to make a hole for the bead strand ¼ inch from the outer edge. See the photograph *right* for details.

Using the smaller pattern, cut a star from a sheet of double-stick adhesive paper. Remove the backing and center it over the blue star. Coat the top adhesive with mica snow or glitter.

String beads onto head and eye pins. Loop the end of the pin through the punched hole.

# pretty pouches

Silk gift bags plumped with gelt during Hanukkah are pretty enough for jewelry or other items the rest of the year.

To make each bag, tear one edge of silk dupioni fabric. Cut the fabric to measure 8×11 inches with one 11-inch side on the torn edge. With right sides facing, fold the fabric so the short sides meet. Sew and overcast the side and bottom edges, leaving the top edge open. Turn the pouch right side out.

Enlarge the star pattern on *page* 157 to scale and cut a star from silver card stock. Emboss the star edges with embossing ink, silver embossing powder, and an embossing gun according to the manufacturer's directions. Write the recipient's name in the center of the star.

Punch a small hole in one point of the star. Thread ribbon through the hole and tie the bag closed.

**Getting Punchy:** Pull that punch bowl off the shelf and let it sparkle as a centerpiece. Place moistened florist's foam in the bottom; use florist's tape to hold it in place if needed. Center a single amaryllis in the foam, then add soft branches of cedar or other greenery. Top it all with acrylic ice cubes, which echo the facets cut into the punch bowl.

# In a Twinkling:
# tabletop

**Bright Dining:** Create custom serving pieces using wooden plates and vibrant decoupage papers. Sand and paint the plate. Cut large images from decoupage papers and adhere them to the plate with decoupage medium. Finish with several coats of gloss sealer. NOTE: Use the plates only for serving dry food; do not use eating utensils on the plates.

**Vine Lines:** Bittersweet vines wind among candles and gourds for a nature-inspired centerpiece. Use a wooden plank for the base, then arrange the elements so the vines intertwine but stay well away from candle flames. Carry the fall theme forward by tying narrow velvet ribbons around napkins, then slipping a clean dried leaf under the ribbon.

▶ Table Wreaths: Red carnations ring a simple hurricane in a series of tabletop wreaths. Soak a floral foam wreath in water until saturated, then place it on a plate or platter several inches larger than the wreath. Clip the stems from carnations and insert the buds into the wreath until it is completely covered. Add small white pre-wired ornaments if desired.

▲ Veggie Platter: Turn to fall's bounty for an impromptu centerpiece. Select various sizes of candles in rich colors, then select complimentary vegetables such as squash, artichokes, tomatillos, red cabbage, and Brussels sprouts. Fill small florist's vials with small bouquets of flowers. Core most of the vegetables, matching the holes to the candle and vial sizes. Arrange the vegetables in a shallow bowl, add some pillar candles, and put the taper candles and flowers in place. Make sure everything is level and sturdy. Never leave burning candles unattended. The centerpiece should last several days at room temperature.

▲ Little Inklings: A collection of inkwells holds sprigs of greenery, flowers, and candles for a casual centerpiece. If inkwells aren't available, look for small old or reproduction bottles to serve the same purpose. Make sure the candles fit tightly and never leave burning candles unattended.

Roast Duckling with
Maple-Cider Glaze

# variations on the

Whether you're serving four—or many more—we have just the right bird for your holiday dinner. Choose game hens for four, duck or capon for eight, or turkey for twelve to fourteen. Succulent side dishes come in two sizes—just right for serving a few couples or a crowd.

## Roast Duckling with Maple-Cider Glaze

*For a special touch, serve chutney in hollowed out orange halves.*

    2  4- to 6-pound domestic
          ducklings
    4  cups apple cider
    2  tablespoons snipped fresh sage
    2  tablespoons maple syrup
       Chicken broth (optional)
    ½  cup apple cider
    2  tablespoons brandy
    1  tablespoon cornstarch
    1  tablespoon snipped fresh sage
    1  recipe Cranberry-Fig
          Chutney (optional)
       Apple slices (optional)
       Fresh sage leaves (optional)

**Rinse** inside of ducklings; pat dry with paper towels. Pull neck skin to back; fasten with skewer. Tie drumsticks to tail. Twist wing tips under back. Place ducklings, breast side up, on rack in a large shallow roasting pan. Prick skin generously with a fork. Sprinkle with salt and freshly ground black pepper. Roast, uncovered, in a 350°F oven for 1½ to 2 hours or until the drumsticks move easily in their sockets (180°F).

**For glaze,** in a large saucepan bring 4 cups cider to boiling. Boil rapidly, uncovered, about 30 minutes or until thickened and reduced to ⅔ cup (mixture will be the consistency of thin syrup). Remove from heat. Stir in 2 tablespoons sage and maple syrup. Brush glaze over ducklings the last 30 minutes of roasting. Cover; let stand for 15 minutes before carving.

**For sauce,** reserve pan drippings. Skim and discard fat from drippings. You should have 1 to 1½ cups drippings (add broth, if necessary, to make 1½ cups). If desired, strain drippings through a fine mesh sieve. Place drippings in a medium saucepan. In a bowl combine ½ cup cider, the brandy, and cornstarch; add to drippings in saucepan. Cook and stir until thickened and bubbly. Cook and stir for 2 minutes more. Stir in the 1 tablespoon sage and season to taste with salt and freshly ground black pepper.

**To carve duckling,** remove the skin if desired. Using a sharp knife, cut duckling along the backbone. Cut downward, removing meat from ribs. Remove wings and legs. Slice breast meat. Serve duck with sauce and, if desired, Cranberry-Fig Chutney. If desired, garnish with apple slices and sage leaves. Makes 8 servings.

**CRANBERRY-FIG CHUTNEY:** In a medium saucepan stir together 2 cups fresh cranberries; 2 cups chopped, peeled apple; 1 cup apple cider; ½ cup snipped dried figs; ¼ cup packed brown sugar; and ¼ teaspoon ground ginger. Bring to boiling; reduce heat. Simmer, uncovered, for 10 to 15 minutes or until thickened. Makes about 3¼ cups.

65

*duckling myths and facts*

Mention duck to the noninitiated, and three myths often come up.

1. Duck's so hard to cook! If you can roast a turkey, you can roast a duck. About the only difference is you'll usually need to prick or score the skin (see instructions *left*).

2. Duck's so fatty! It's true that duck has a luscious, fatty skin that avid duck lovers cherish. Skin aside, however, most duck you can buy in America are chosen and bred for leanness.

3. Duck's so "gamey"! White Pekin, the breed of duck that's most widely available at supermarkets in the United States, has a more mild flavor than other breeds such as Muscovy and Moulard. The mildness adapts to many flavors and styles of preparation, which explains why it's so popular at contemporary bistros, where chefs put their own spin on the bird.

# holiday bird

## Green Beans and Carrots with Citrus-Hazelnut Gremolata

*Hint: If desired, replace the fresh beans with frozen haricorts verts (thin whole green beans).*

- 1 pound fresh green beans, trimmed
- 1½ cups packaged julienned carrots
- 2 tablespoons finely chopped toasted hazelnuts (filberts)* or almonds
- 2 tablespoons snipped fresh Italian (flat-leaf) parsley
- 1½ teaspoons finely shredded orange peel
- 1 teaspoon finely shredded lemon peel
- ½ teaspoon finely shredded lime peel
- 1 tablespoon butter
- 1 tablespoon olive oil
- 1 shallot, finely chopped
- 2 cloves garlic, minced
- ¼ teaspoon salt
- ⅛ teaspoon ground black pepper

**In a 4-quart Dutch oven** cook the beans and carrots, uncovered, in enough lightly salted boiling water to cover about 10 minutes or until tender; drain and set vegetables aside.

**For gremolata,** in a small bowl stir together nuts, parsley, orange peel, lemon peel, and lime peel; set aside.

**In the same pan** heat butter and oil over medium-high heat. Add shallot and garlic; cook and stir for 1 to 2 minutes or until shallot is tender. Add the beans, carrots, salt, and pepper. Toss to heat through. Transfer vegetable mixture to a serving dish. Sprinkle with gremolata. Makes 6 to 8 servings.

**\*NOTE:** To toast and remove skins from hazelnuts, place nuts in a shallow baking pan. Bake, uncovered, in a 350°F oven for 8 to 10 minutes or until lightly toasted, stirring twice. Turn hot hazelnuts out onto a clean kitchen towel; cool slightly. Gently roll in towel to remove skins.

**TO MAKE AHEAD:** Prepare gremolata ahead. Cover and chill up to 4 hours.

**FOR 12 TO 14 SERVINGS:** Prepare as above, except use a 6-quart Dutch oven and double all ingredients.

## Peas Parisienne

- 1 cup finely chopped onion (1 large)
- 1 tablespoon minced garlic (about 6 cloves)
- 1 teaspoon snipped fresh thyme or ¼ teaspoon dried thyme, crushed
- 2 tablespoons butter
- 1 16-ounce package frozen peas
- ¼ teaspoon ground black pepper
  Pinch ground nutmeg
- 1 cup chicken broth
- 2½ cups chopped romaine

**In a large saucepan** cook onion, garlic, and thyme in hot butter over medium heat about 5 minutes or until onion softens and begins to color slightly.

**Add peas,** pepper, and nutmeg. Add broth. Bring to boiling; reduce heat. Simmer 5 minutes or until heated through. Add romaine and cook for 1 minute more or until romaine is wilted. Transfer to a serving bowl. Makes 8 servings.

**FOR 12 TO 16 SERVINGS:** Prepare as above, except use a 4-quart Dutch oven; 2 cups finely chopped onion; 1 tablespoon minced garlic; 2 teaspoons snipped fresh thyme or ½ teaspoon dried thyme, crushed; ¼ cup butter; two 16-ounce packages frozen peas; ½ teaspoon ground black pepper; ⅛ teaspoon ground nutmeg; 2 cups chicken broth; and 5 cups chopped romaine.

*Green Beans and Carrots with Citrus-Hazelnut Gremolata*

# Citrus Tapenade Game Hens

*Game hens have a reputation for being impressive, but they're as easy as can be to roast. A flavorful tapenade tucked under the skin is well worth the trouble. Hint: To split the hens, thaw if frozen, then use a kitchen shears to cut the hens in half.*

½ cup finely chopped pitted
    niçoise or kalamata olives
1 tablespoon capers, drained and
    finely chopped
1 clove garlic, minced
1 teaspoon anchovy
    paste (optional)
½ teaspoon finely shredded
    orange peel
1 tablespoon olive oil
2 1¼- to 1½-pound Cornish
    game hens, split in halves
    lengthwise
1 tablespoon olive oil
  Salt
  Freshly ground black pepper
2 tablespoons finely chopped
    shallots
1 cup dry white wine or
    dry vermouth
¼ cup chicken broth
1 tablespoon butter
1 tablespoon snipped fresh thyme
  Fresh thyme sprigs

**For tapenade,** in a small bowl combine olives, capers, garlic, anchovy paste (if using), and orange peel. Stir in 1 tablespoon olive oil.

**Rinse** inside of hens; pat dry with paper towels. Loosen skin on hens. Using your fingers, carefully spread tapenade evenly under skin of each hen half. Brush hens with 1 tablespoon olive oil and sprinkle both sides of hen halves with salt and pepper. Arrange hens, cut side down, in a large ovenproof skillet. Roast, uncovered, in a 425°F oven

*Citrus Tapenade Game Hens and Peas Parisienne*

about 35 minutes or until no pink remains and a meat thermometer inserted in the thigh registers 180°F. (Thermometer should not touch bone.) Remove hens to a warm platter. Cover to keep warm.

**Drain** all but about 1 tablespoon drippings from skillet. Add shallots to skillet; cook and stir over medium heat for 2 to 3 minutes or until shallots are tender. Remove skillet from heat. Add wine and broth. Return skillet to heat.

Cook and stir to loosen browned bits from skillet. Bring mixture to boiling; reduce heat. Simmer, uncovered, for 4 to 5 minutes to reduce slightly. (Should have about ½ cup of sauce.) Remove skillet from heat and whisk in butter until melted. Stir in snipped thyme. Spoon sauce over hens. If desired, garnish with thyme sprigs. Makes 4 servings.

*Herb-Roasted Capon with*
*Caramelized Onions*

# Herb-Roasted Capon with Caramelized Onions

*A capon is characteristically a plump and juicy bird. Bigger than a chicken, smaller than a turkey, it's perfect when you're serving eight to ten.*

 2 teaspoons dried thyme, crushed
 1 teaspoon dried marjoram, crushed
 1 teaspoon dried savory, crushed
 ½ teaspoon dried lavender, crushed
 ½ teaspoon celery salt
 1 7- to 8-pound capon or roasting chicken
　 Olive oil or cooking oil
 2 tablespoons butter
 4 cups thin red or white onion wedges
 2 cups pearl onions, peeled
 1 tablespoon packed brown sugar
 2 tablespoons balsamic vinegar

**In a small bowl** stir together thyme, marjoram, savory, lavender, and celery salt; remove 1 tablespoon of the mixture and set aside. Rinse inside of capon; pat dry with paper towels. Loosen skin from breast of capon; rub the remaining herb mixture over meat under breast skin and inside cavity of capon.

**Twist wing tips** under back. Tie drumsticks to tail. Place capon, breast side up, on a rack in a shallow roasting pan. Brush bird with oil. Insert an oven-going meat thermometer into the center of one of the inside thigh muscles. (Thermometer should not touch bone.) Roast, uncovered, in a 350°F oven for 2 to 2½ hours or until bird is nearly done. Sprinkle reserved herb mixture over entire bird. Return to oven and roast about 15 minutes more or until thermometer registers 180°F.

**Meanwhile,** 20 minutes before bird is done, in a 12-inch skillet melt butter over medium heat. Add onion wedges, pearl onions, and brown sugar. Cook, covered, for 20 to 30 minutes or until onions are very tender; stir occasionally.

**Transfer capon** to a serving platter, reserving juices in pan. Cover and let capon stand for 15 minutes before carving. Pour pan juices into a glass measuring cup. Skim off fat and discard. Measure ¼ cup juices; discard remaining juices. Wipe out roasting pan with paper towels. Place onion mixture in same roasting pan; add juices and vinegar and toss to coat. Roast, uncovered, for 15 minutes. Serve capon with onions. Makes 8 to 10 servings.

# Potato-Brie Gratin

✳

*Take scalloped potatoes to the next level! White potatoes, sweet potatoes, and Brie—melded together with a rich white sauce—stack up to an opulent side dish.*

 1 pound white or baking potatoes, peeled and sliced
 1 pound sweet potatoes, peeled and sliced
 2 shallots, finely chopped
 1 tablespoon butter
 1 tablespoon all-purpose flour
 ¼ teaspoon salt
 ⅛ teaspoon ground black pepper
 1¼ cups half-and-half, light cream, or milk
 1 8-ounce package Brie cheese (rind removed, if desired), sliced
 1½ cups cubed country-style French or Italian bread
 2 tablespoons finely shredded Parmesan cheese
 2 tablespoons butter, melted
 1 tablespoon snipped fresh lemon-thyme or thyme or 1 teaspoon dried thyme, crushed

**Grease** a 2-quart au gratin or baking dish; set aside. Place a large steamer basket in a large skillet or 4-quart Dutch oven with a tight-fitting lid. Add water to just below the basket. Bring water to boiling. Add potatoes to basket (in batches, if necessary), keeping sweet potatoes and white potatoes as separate as possible. Cover and steam for 10 minutes (potatoes will not be fully tender). Remove from basket and set aside to cool.

**Meanwhile,** for sauce, in a medium saucepan cook shallots in the 1 tablespoon butter until tender. Stir in flour, salt, and pepper until combined. Add half-and-half all at once. Cook and stir until slightly thickened and bubbly; set aside.

68

**Layer half** of the cooled white potatoes and half of the cooled sweet potatoes in prepared dish, alternating sweet and white potatoes as desired. Arrange Brie slices over potatoes. Top with remaining potatoes, alternating as desired. Slowly pour sauce over layers. If desired, cover and chill up to 24 hours. **Bake,** covered, in a 350°F oven* for 15 minutes (20 minutes if chilled).

**Meanwhile,** in a medium bowl toss together bread cubes, Parmesan cheese, the 2 tablespoons melted butter, and thyme. Uncover potato mixture and top evenly with bread cube mixture. Bake, uncovered, for 15 minutes more (20 minutes if chilled) or until bubbly and potatoes are tender. Let stand 10 minutes before serving. Serves 6 to 8.

*****NOTE:** For a 325°F oven, bake layered mixture, covered, for 20 minutes (25 minutes if chilled). Top with bread cube mixture. Bake, uncovered, for 20 minutes more (25 minutes if chilled) or until bubbly and potatoes are tender. Let stand 10 minutes before serving.

**FOR 12 TO 14 SERVINGS:** Prepare as above, except use a large saucepan to prepare the sauce and grease a 3- to 3½-quart au gratin or baking dish. Use 2 pounds white or baking potatoes; 2 pounds sweet potatoes; 4 shallots, chopped; 2 tablespoons butter; 2 tablespoons all-purpose flour; ½ teaspoon salt; ¼ teaspoon ground black pepper; 2½ cups half-and-half, light cream, or milk; two 8-ounce packages Brie cheese; 3 cups cubed country-style French or Italian bread; ¼ cup finely shredded Parmesan cheese; ¼ cup butter, melted; and 2 tablespoons snipped fresh lemon-thyme or thyme or 2 teaspoons dried thyme, crushed.

**Bake,** covered, in a 350°F oven for 20 minutes (25 minutes if chilled), then uncover and bake 20 minutes (25 minutes if chilled) or until bubbly and potatoes are tender. Let stand as above. For a 325°F oven, bake, covered, for 25 minutes (30 minutes if chilled), then uncover and bake 25 minutes (30 to 35 minutes if chilled) or until bubbly and potatoes are tender. Let stand as above.

---

# Turkey with Roasted Garlic Gravy

*The wonderful mellow-sweet flavor of the roasted garlic brings a gourmet edge to an otherwise tradition-bound bird.*
*Note: Straining the gravy is a matter of taste—some like the bits of roasted garlic and sage studded throughout, others prefer a smoother gravy.*

    1  8- to 12-pound turkey
    2  tablespoons olive oil
    1  teaspoon salt
    ½  teaspoon freshly ground
         black pepper
    1  head garlic
    ¼  cup all-purpose flour
    1  14-ounce can chicken broth
    1  tablespoon snipped fresh sage
         or 1½ teaspoons dried sage,
         crushed
       Salt
       Freshly ground black pepper

**Remove** neck and giblets from body and neck cavities of turkey. Rinse inside of turkey; pat dry with paper towels. Pull neck skin to back of turkey; fasten with a skewer. Tuck the ends of the drumsticks under the band of skin across the tail. If there is no band of skin, tie drumsticks to tail. Twist wing tips under back.

**Place turkey,** breast side up, on a rack in a shallow roasting pan. Brush with oil and sprinkle with the 1 teaspoon salt and the ½ teaspoon pepper. Insert an oven-going meat thermometer into the center of one of the inside thigh muscles. (Thermometer should not touch bone.)

Cover turkey loosely with foil. Roast in a 325°F oven for 2¾ to 3 hours.

**Wrap garlic** in foil and place next to turkey in oven. Roast garlic for 1 hour or until soft. Remove from oven and set garlic aside.

**During the last 45 minutes** of roasting, remove foil from turkey. Cut band of skin or string between drumsticks so thighs cook evenly. Roast until the thermometer registers 180°F. The juices should run clear and the drumsticks should move easily in their sockets. Remove turkey from oven. Cover and let stand 15 to 20 minutes before carving.

**Meanwhile, for gravy,** scrape drippings and browned bits from roasting pan into a glass measuring cup. Let stand 5 minutes or until fat rises to the top. Skim off fat and discard. Cut ½ inch off top of roasted garlic and squeeze the pulp from cloves into a small bowl. With a fork, mash the garlic until almost smooth; set aside. In a small bowl stir flour and ¼ cup of the broth until smooth.

**In a small saucepan** combine the reserved drippings, garlic, and sage. Bring to boiling over medium heat. Slowly whisk in flour mixture and remaining 1½ cups broth. Cook and stir over medium heat until mixture is thickened and bubbly. Cook and stir for 2 minutes more. Remove from heat. Season to taste with additional salt and pepper. If desired, strain gravy mixture through a fine mesh strainer to remove bits of garlic and sage. Carve turkey. Serve with gravy. Makes 12 to 14 servings.

69

Smoked Salmon Pasta Bake

# bring a
beautiful dish

Holiday time is potluck time. But not just any potluck recipe will do during this season of celebrations. When it's your turn to bring a dish, choose from this selection of head-turning appetizers, entrées, sides, and desserts and serve a house-full in style.

## Smoked Salmon Pasta Bake

*When you take a basic pasta bake to a whole new level by adding smoked salmon, the result is a dish worthy of a champagne toast.*

  1  pound crimini or button mushrooms, sliced ¼ inch thick
  2  tablespoons olive oil
      Salt
      Ground black pepper
  1  16-ounce package dried mostaccioli, penne, or farfalle (about 5½ cups)
  ⅓  cup finely chopped shallots
  ¼  cup butter
  ¼  cup all-purpose flour
  ¼  teaspoon salt
  ⅛  teaspoon cayenne pepper
      Dash ground nutmeg
  4  cups half-and-half, light cream, or milk
1½  cups shredded Gruyère or Swiss cheese (6 ounces)
  ¾  cup finely shredded Parmesan cheese (3 ounces)
  8  ounces smoked salmon (not lox), with skin and bones removed
  ½  cup chopped fresh Italian (flat-leaf) parsley
  1  cup soft bread crumbs (about 1½ slices bread)
  2  tablespoons butter, melted

**To roast mushrooms,** place them in a shallow roasting pan. Drizzle with oil and sprinkle with salt and black pepper; toss to coat. Roast, uncovered, in a 425°F oven for 20 to 25 minutes or until most of the liquid has evaporated, stirring once or twice; set aside. In a large saucepan cook pasta according to package directions; drain. Return pasta to saucepan; set aside.

**Meanwhile,** for sauce, in a medium saucepan cook and stir shallots in ¼ cup butter over medium heat for 2 to 3 minutes or until tender. Stir in flour, the ¼ teaspoon salt, cayenne pepper, and nutmeg. Cook and stir for 1 minute more. Add half-and-half all at once. Cook and stir until thickened and bubbly. Reduce heat to low. Add Gruyère and Parmesan cheeses; stir until cheeses melt.

**Stir sauce,** roasted mushrooms, salmon, and parsley into cooked pasta. Spoon mixture into a 3-quart rectangular baking dish or divide mixture evenly among 10 to 12 (6- to 8-ounce each) ramekins or custard cups.

**Bake,** covered, in a 350°F oven for 25 minutes (15 minutes for ramekins).

**Meanwhile,** in a small bowl combine bread crumbs and the 2 tablespoons melted butter. Uncover pasta mixture and sprinkle bread crumb mixture evenly over pasta. Bake, uncovered, for 5 to 10 minutes more or until crumbs are golden and mixture is heated through. Makes 10 to 12 servings.

## Corn and Polenta Bake

  4  fresh ears of corn or 2 cups frozen whole kernel corn
  1  cup chopped green sweet pepper
  ½  cup chopped onion
  2  cloves garlic, minced
¼ to ½  teaspoon coarsely ground black pepper
  2  tablespoons cooking oil
  2  16-ounce tubes refrigerated cooked polenta
  6  slightly beaten eggs
  1  tablespoon stone-ground mustard or Dijon-style mustard
  1  teaspoon sugar
  ¾  teaspoon salt
1½  cups soft bread crumbs
  2  tablespoons butter, melted

**Lightly grease** a 2-quart rectangular baking dish; set aside. If using fresh corn, cut kernels from ears (you should have about 2 cups). In a large saucepan cook corn, sweet pepper, onion, garlic, and black pepper in hot oil about 5 minutes or until just tender.

**Crumble polenta** (you should have about 7 cups); set aside. In a large bowl combine eggs, mustard, sugar, and salt. Stir in cooked vegetable mixture and the polenta. Spoon into prepared dish.

**In a small bowl** combine crumbs and butter. Sprinkle over polenta mixture. Bake in a 325°F oven about 50 minutes or until a knife inserted near center comes out clean. Makes 12 servings.

*Deviled Eggs with
Shrimp*

# Rustic Gremolata Potatoes

*Your holiday-dinner hosts are going to
love it when you say you'll bring the
side-dish potatoes. They'll appreciate your
sparing them the last-minute boiling and
mashing. Tote the taters in the slow
cooker to free up coveted space on the
stovetop and in the oven.*

  4  pounds small red potatoes,
     quartered
  1  8-ounce package cream
     cheese, softened and cut into
     chunks
  1  8-ounce carton light dairy sour
     cream
  1  cup finely shredded Vella Jack
     (Dry Jack) cheese or Asiago
     cheese (4 ounces)
$1/2$  cup half-and-half, light cream,
     or milk
     Salt
     Freshly ground black pepper
$1/4$  cup chopped fresh Italian
     (flat-leaf) parsley
  1  tablespoon finely shredded
     lemon peel
  2  cloves garlic, minced

**In a 4- to 5-quart Dutch oven** cook
potatoes in enough lightly salted boiling
water to cover for 15 to 20 minutes or
until tender; drain. Return potatoes to
Dutch oven. Add cream cheese, sour
cream, shredded cheese, and half-and-
half. Coarsely mash with a potato
masher. Season with salt and pepper to
taste. If potatoes seem dry, stir in a little
milk or additional sour cream.

**To keep** potatoes warm, place mashed
potatoes in a 4- to 5-quart slow cooker
on low-heat setting for up to 2 hours.

**For gremolata topping,** in a small
bowl combine parsley, lemon peel, and
garlic. At serving time, top each serving
of potatoes with gremolata mixture.
Makes 10 to 12 servings.

# Deviled Eggs with Shrimp

*Deviled eggs are no stranger to the buffet
table. Dress them up for the holidays with
a little shrimp and a dollop of caviar.
Hint: Be sure the caviar is chilled and add
it just before serving; otherwise, the color
may bleed into eggs.*

 12  hard-cooked eggs
  3  tablespoons mayonnaise or
     salad dressing
  3  tablespoons dairy sour cream
  1  tablespoon snipped fresh
     tarragon or 1 teaspoon dried
     tarragon, crushed

  2  teaspoons Dijon-style mustard
$1/4$  teaspoon cayenne pepper
$1/2$  cup chopped cooked shrimp
     Black lumpfish caviar, black
     mustard seeds, or poppy
     seeds (optional)

**Halve** the hard-cooked eggs lengthwise
and remove yolks. Set whites aside.
Place yolks in a bowl; mash with a fork.
Add mayonnaise, sour cream, tarragon,
mustard, and cayenne pepper; mix well.
Gently stir in shrimp.

**Stuff egg white halves** with yolk
mixture. Cover and chill up to
24 hours. If desired, garnish with caviar,
black mustard seeds, or poppy seeds
before serving. Makes 24 appetizers.

# Onion-Olive Tart (Pissaladière)

*This famous South-of-France specialty is great for potlucks, as there's no need to rush it from oven to buffet table. The flavors are actually at their peak when served at room temperature. Serve as an appetizer with a selection of artisanal cheeses.*

- ¼ cup olive oil
- 5 cups sliced onions
- ½ teaspoon dried thyme, crushed
- ¼ teaspoon freshly ground black pepper
- 2 large cloves garlic, minced
- 2 2-ounce cans anchovy fillets, drained
- 1 16-ounce loaf frozen white or wheat bread dough, thawed
- ½ cup finely shredded Parmesan cheese (2 ounces)
- ½ cup pitted ripe olives, halved

**In a large skillet** heat 2 tablespoons of the oil over medium-low heat. Add onions, thyme, and pepper; cook about 30 minutes or until onions are very tender and golden brown; stir occasionally. Remove from heat; set aside.

**In a small bowl** combine the garlic and remaining 2 tablespoons oil. Mash 6 of the anchovies and stir into the oil mixture. Cut remaining anchovies into thin strips; set aside.

**Grease** a very large baking sheet; set aside. On a lightly floured surface, roll bread dough into a 12-inch square. (If dough seems too elastic, let it rest for a few minutes.) Transfer to prepared baking sheet; reshape if necessary.

**Brush with garlic mixture;** sprinkle evenly with ¼ cup of the Parmesan. Spread onions evenly over dough; sprinkle with remaining Parmesan. Top with anchovy strips and olives.

**Bake in a 450°F oven** for 12 to 15 minutes or until crust is golden brown. Serve warm or cooled to room temperature. Cut into squares to serve. Makes 36 appetizers.

# Marjoram-Berry Tarts

*The tiny, tart red lingonberry is a member of the cranberry family. Typically sold in jars as sweet sauces or preserves, they partner well with dried cranberries in miniature phyllo shells.*

- 2 2.1-ounce packages baked mini phyllo dough shells (30 total)
- 1 14-ounce jar lingonberries
- ⅓ cup snipped dried cranberries
- 1 slightly beaten egg
- 2 tablespoons honey
- ¾ teaspoon snipped fresh marjoram or ¼ teaspoon dried marjoram, crushed
- ½ teaspoon vanilla
- ¼ teaspoon ground ginger or ground cinnamon
- ½ cup dairy sour cream (optional)
- 1 tablespoon packed brown sugar (optional)
- ¼ cup sliced almonds, toasted (optional)
  Fresh marjoram sprigs (optional)

**Place phyllo dough shells** on a large ungreased baking sheet; set aside.

**For filling,** in a medium bowl stir together lingonberries, cranberries, egg, honey, marjoram, vanilla, and ginger. Spoon a slightly rounded tablespoon of filling into each phyllo shell.

**Bake, uncovered,** in a 350°F oven for 20 minutes or until filling is bubbly. Transfer to a wire rack; cool.

**Meanwhile,** if desired, in a small bowl combine sour cream and brown sugar. Top each tart with sour cream mixture. If desired, sprinkle with almonds and garnish with sprigs of fresh marjoram. Makes 30 tarts.

**To Make Ahead:** Place baked phyllo shells in an airtight container; cover. Store at room temperature for up to 1 day. Place the filling in an airtight container; cover. Store in the refrigerator for up to 1 day. Fill, bake, and cool tarts before serving.

*Marjoram-Berry Tarts*

# Roasted Vegetable Phyllo Bake

*Treat vegetarians to something wonderful with this beautiful bake.*

3 red and/or yellow sweet peppers, halved, stems removed, and seeded

3 large onions, thickly sliced and separated into rings

10 cloves garlic, peeled

¼ cup olive oil

¼ cup chicken broth or vegetable broth

2 teaspoons herbes de Provence

1 pound fresh asparagus spears, trimmed

1 pound fresh mushrooms, such as brown, shiitake, portobello, and/or white button, thickly sliced

1⅓ cups olive oil

1 16-ounce package frozen phyllo dough (14×9-inch rectangles), thawed

2 4-ounce logs goat cheese (chèvre)

**Place pepper halves,** cut side down, on a foil-lined baking sheet. In a large bowl combine onions, garlic, and 1 tablespoon of the olive oil; toss to combine. Spread mixture in a 15×10×1-inch baking pan. Sprinkle with salt and freshly ground black pepper. Roast pepper halves and onion mixture at the same time on 2 racks in a 425°F oven until pepper skins are blistered and dark and onions are starting to brown; stir onion mixture once or twice. Allow 20 to 25 minutes for peppers; 30 to 35 minutes for onions.

**Carefully bring** foil around pepper halves to enclose. Let stand about 15 minutes or until peppers are cool enough to handle. Unwrap foil; remove and discard skin from peppers. Coarsely chop peppers; set aside.

**Place onion mixture** in a food processor or blender; add broth. Process or blend until finely chopped (mixture will be partially pureed). Stir in herbes de Provence and chopped peppers.

**Meanwhile,** in a shallow roasting pan toss asparagus with 1 tablespoon of the olive oil; sprinkle with salt and black pepper. In a shallow roasting pan or 13×9×2-inch baking pan toss mushrooms with 2 tablespoons olive oil; sprinkle with salt and black pepper.

**Roast mushrooms** and asparagus at the same time on 2 racks in oven until browned, stirring once or twice. Allow 15 to 20 minutes for asparagus; 20 to 25 minutes for mushrooms. Set aside to cool. Coarsely chop asparagus. Stir asparagus and mushrooms into onion mixture; set aside.

**To assemble,** brush the bottom of a 13×9×2-inch baking pan or 3-quart rectangular baking dish with some of the 1⅓ cups olive oil. Unfold phyllo dough. Work with 1 sheet of phyllo at a time, keeping remaining sheets covered with plastic wrap until needed. Layer 15 phyllo sheets in the pan, brushing each sheet lightly with oil before adding next sheet. Spread half of the roasted vegetable mixture over phyllo layers. Crumble half of the goat cheese on top of vegetable layer. Repeat the layering of 15 more phyllo sheets, brushing lightly with oil between each sheet. Top with remaining vegetables and goat cheese. Layer remaining phyllo sheets on top, brushing lightly with oil between each.

**With a sharp knife,** cut into 12 squares. Bake in a 375°F oven for 35 to 40 minutes or until top is golden brown. Makes 12 servings.

**TO MAKE AHEAD:** Prepare vegetables as above up to assembling. Cover; chill up to 24 hours. Assemble; bake as above.

*Roasted Vegetable Phyllo Bake*

# Three-Cheese and Artichoke Lasagna

*Lasagna usually makes for great potluck fare—but it's rarely thought of as particularly elegant. Here, artichokes, smoked meat, and white wine raise the dish to a regal level.*

Three-Cheese and
Artichoke Lasagna

12 dried lasagna noodles
 1 9-ounce package frozen artichoke hearts, thawed, or one 14-ounce can artichoke hearts, drained
 1 tablespoon butter or olive oil
 1 cup finely chopped red onion
 4 cloves garlic, minced
 ½ cup dry white wine
 1¾ cups half-and-half, light cream, or milk
 3 tablespoons all-purpose flour
 1 teaspoon dried tarragon, crushed
 1 teaspoon finely shredded lemon peel
 ½ teaspoon salt
 ¼ teaspoon ground black pepper
 1 15-ounce container ricotta cheese
 ¾ cup finely shredded Parmigiano-Reggiano, Asiago, or Parmesan cheese (3 ounces)
 1½ cups shredded Gruyère cheese (6 ounces)
 8 ounces smoked boneless turkey breast or cooked ham, coarsely chopped

**Cook noodles** according to package directions. Drain and rinse with cold water; drain again. Set aside. Quarter artichoke hearts lengthwise; set aside. Lightly grease a 3-quart rectangular baking dish; set aside.

**Meanwhile,** for sauce, in a medium saucepan melt butter over medium heat. Add onion and garlic; cook about 5 minutes or until onion is tender, stirring occasionally. Remove saucepan from heat; carefully add wine. Return saucepan to heat; bring to boiling. Boil gently, uncovered, for 3 minutes.

**In a small bowl** whisk together half-and-half, flour, tarragon, lemon peel, salt, and pepper; stir into onion mixture. Cook and stir until thickened and bubbly. Stir in artichokes; set aside.

**In a medium bowl** stir together ricotta cheese and ¼ cup of the Parmigiano-Reggiano cheese; set aside.

**Spread** one-fourth of the sauce (about ¾ cup) in the bottom of the prepared baking dish. Layer 4 of the noodles, half of the Gruyère cheese, and half of the smoked turkey on top of the sauce. Dollop half of the ricotta mixture on top and drizzle with another one-fourth of the sauce (about ¾ cup). Spread evenly. Repeat layering once, starting with noodles. Top with remaining noodles; spread remaining sauce on top of the noodles.

**Bake,** covered, in a 375°F oven for 20 minutes. Uncover and sprinkle with the remaining ½ cup Parmigiano-Reggiano cheese. Bake, uncovered, about 20 minutes more or until heated through. Let stand for 15 minutes before serving. Makes 12 servings.

**To Make Ahead:** Prepare lasagna as directed except do not bake. Cover and chill up to 24 hours along with the remaining ½ cup Parmigiano-Reggiano cheese. To serve, bake, covered, in a 375°F oven for 30 minutes. Uncover and top with cheese. Bake, uncovered, for 35 to 40 minutes more or until heated through. Let stand for 15 minutes before serving.

## toting tips

With food safety in mind, follow these tips when toting foods to potlucks.

KEEP COLD FOODS COLD

Chill a cooler by filling it with ice for at least 30 minutes before packing it. Make sure the food is chilled, and pack it in the cooler just before leaving home. Surround the food with ice. Cold foods should be kept at 40°F or colder. You can keep foods cold by nesting dishes in bowls of ice.

KEEP HOT FOODS HOT

Time the making of your recipe so the food finishes cooking just before you head for the potluck. Cover the dish tightly with foil and wrap it in layers of newspaper or a heavy towel. Place the dish in an insulated cooler, insulated casserole carrier, or basket with warming bricks. Once at your destination, hot foods should be kept at 140°F or warmer. On the buffet table you can keep hot foods hot with chafing dishes, slow cookers, and warming trays.

THE TWO-HOUR RULE

Do not allow foods to sit at room temperature for more than 2 hours. Discard any foods that have sat at room temperature for longer.

*Baked Appetizer Crepes*

# Baked Appetizer Crepes

*Choose this recipe when the tone of the potluck will be formal. Or serve it with a tart green salad as a main dish for six.*

12  6-inch Basic Crepes
2  beaten eggs
2  cups ricotta cheese (15 ounces)
1½  cups shredded Swiss cheese
  (6 ounces)
1  10-ounce package frozen
  chopped spinach, thawed
  and well drained
1½  cups soft bread crumbs
  (2 slices bread)
½  cup grated Parmesan cheese
¼  teaspoon ground black pepper
  Dash garlic powder
½  cup butter
1  cup whipping cream
½  cup grated Parmesan cheese

**Prepare Basic Crepes.** For filling, in a bowl combine eggs, ricotta cheese, Swiss cheese, spinach, bread crumbs, ½ cup Parmesan cheese, pepper, and garlic powder; mix well. Spoon about ⅓ cup filling into center of each crepe; roll up. Cut each rolled crepe crosswise into thirds. Place the pieces, cut side up, in a 2-quart baking dish (placing pieces close together will help them remain upright).

**For sauce,** in a small saucepan melt butter; stir in cream and the ½ cup Parmesan cheese. Cook and stir over medium heat until mixture thickens slightly. Pour the sauce over crepes. Bake in a 400°F oven for 18 to 20 minutes or until heated through. Makes 36 appetizers.

**BASIC CREPES:** In a bowl combine 2 beaten eggs, 1½ cups milk, 1 cup all-purpose flour, 1 tablespoon cooking oil, and ¼ teaspoon salt; beat until combined. Heat a lightly greased 6-inch skillet over medium-high heat; remove from heat. Spoon in 2 tablespoons batter; lift and tilt skillet to spread batter. Return to heat; cook for 2 to 3 minutes or until brown on 1 side only. (Or cook on a crepe maker according to manufacturer's directions.) Invert skillet over paper towels to remove crepe. Repeat with remaining crepe batter, greasing the skillet occasionally.

# Croque Monsieur Triangles

*Here's a super-easy, never-fail potluck offering everyone will love. This recipe is named for a favorite French café snack: the croque-monsieur sandwich made of melted ham and cheese.*

1  17.3-ounce package frozen puff pastry (2 sheets), thawed
3  tablespoons Dijon-style mustard
4  ounces shaved deli ham*
¾  cup shredded Gruyère or Swiss cheese (3 ounces)
1  egg
1  tablespoon water

**Grease 2 large baking sheets** or line with parchment paper; set aside. Unfold pastry on a lightly floured surface. Roll each sheet into a 12-inch square. Cut each square into nine 4-inch squares.

**Spoon** ½ teaspoon mustard onto center of each square; spread slightly. Place a small pile of ham on mustard. Top evenly with cheese.

**In a small bowl** lightly beat together the egg and water with a fork. Brush edges of squares with egg mixture. Fold a corner of each square over filling to opposite corner, forming a triangle. Press edges with the tines of a fork to seal. Place bundles on prepared baking sheets. Prick tops with a fork. Brush with egg mixture.

**Bake,** uncovered, in a 400°F oven about 12 minutes or until golden. Cool slightly before serving. Makes 18 appetizers.

**\*Note:** Select a distinctly flavored ham such as Virginia ham or country ham.

**To Make Ahead:** Cover filled triangles on each baking sheet with plastic wrap; chill up to 2 hours before baking.

# Lime Pecan Shortbread Bars

*Sometimes at buffets, the dessert table groans under the weight of heavy desserts. Often, something sweet, petite, tart and tingly—like these sprightly citrusy bars— is what party-goers really want.*

2  cups all-purpose flour
½  cup powdered sugar
2  tablespoons cornstarch
¼  teaspoon salt
¾  cup butter
½  cup finely chopped pecans, toasted
4  slightly beaten eggs
4  slightly beaten egg yolks
1⅓  cups granulated sugar
1½  teaspoons finely shredded lime peel
1  cup fresh Key lime juice or lime juice
½  cup butter, cut up
1  recipe Sweetened Mascarpone Cheese (optional)
   Finely shredded lime peel (optional)

**Grease** a 13×9×2-inch baking pan; set aside. For crust, in a large bowl combine the flour, powdered sugar, cornstarch, and salt. Using a pastry blender, cut in ¾ cup butter until the mixture resembles coarse crumbs. Stir in pecans. Press mixture into the bottom of prepared pan. Bake in a 350°F oven for 18 to 20 minutes or until edges are golden. Remove from oven; set aside. Reduce oven temperature to 325°F.

**Meanwhile,** for filling, in a medium saucepan combine eggs, egg yolks, granulated sugar, 1½ teaspoons lime peel, lime juice, and dash salt. Stir in the ½ cup butter. Cook and stir over medium-low heat about 10 minutes or until filling thickens. Remove from heat.

**Pour filling over crust.** (If desired, strain filling over crust through a fine-mesh sieve.) Bake about 10 minutes or until filling is just set. Cool on a wire rack.

Cut into bars. If desired, spoon Sweetened Mascarpone Cheese into a pastry bag fitted with a star tip. Pipe a star onto each cut bar. If desired, sprinkle bars with shredded lime peel. Cover and store in the refrigerator up to 2 days. Makes 36 bars.

**Sweetened Mascarpone Cheese:** Beat together one 8-ounce container mascarpone cheese with ¼ cup powdered sugar.

# Orzo-Shrimp Salad

1  16-ounce package dry orzo
1  12-ounce jar marinated artichoke hearts, drained and coarsely chopped
1  pound cooked, peeled, and deveined medium shrimp
1  medium red onion, halved and thinly sliced (about 1 cup)
½  cup slivered pitted kalamata olives
½  cup chopped fresh Italian (flat-leaf) parsley
4  ounces prosciutto, chopped
1  recipe Orange-Walnut Vinaigrette
4  ounces feta cheese, crumbled
¾  cup chopped walnuts, toasted

**Cook orzo** according to package directions; drain. Rinse with cold water; drain again.

**In a large bowl** combine orzo, artichoke hearts, shrimp, onion, olives, parsley, and prosciutto; toss to combine. Add Orange-Walnut Vinaigrette; toss gently to coat. Cover and chill for 2 to 4 hours. To serve, sprinkle with feta cheese and walnuts. Makes 12 servings.

**Orange-Walnut Vinaigrette:** In a screw-top jar combine 1 cup fresh orange juice; ¼ cup white wine vinegar; ¼ cup walnut oil; 2 cloves garlic, minced; 1 teaspoon Dijon-style mustard; ½ teaspoon salt; and ¼ teaspoon freshly ground black pepper. Cover; shake well.

making music

Spread helpings of holiday cheer this season—invite a chorus of voices to broadcast songs of comfort and joy throughout the neighborhood. Afterwards invite your merry minstrels inside for a musically-themed evening of nibbles. These festive foods, invites, decorations, and party favors strike just the right chord.

*Mini White Chocolate Cheesecakes, page 82*

# and memories

80

# Garlicky Marinated Vegetables

✳

*The marinade here has so much going on that you won't need a dip to go with these vegetables. The recipe tastes best at room temperature, so set it out an hour before you serve, perhaps just before you go on a brief caroling jaunt.*

1/4 cup olive oil

2 tablespoons rice vinegar

1 tablespoon coarse-grain brown mustard

4 cloves garlic, minced

1/2 teaspoon salt

1/4 teaspoon crushed red pepper

1/4 teaspoon coarsely ground black pepper

1 small zucchini, cut into 1/2-inch-thick sticks

1 cup fresh snow pea pods, trimmed

2 medium yellow and/or green sweet peppers, cut into 1/2-inch strips

4 ounces whole button mushrooms, halved (1 1/2 cups)

1 cup pitted kalamata olives

1 cup cherry or grape tomatoes

**For marinade,** in a screw-top jar place oil, vinegar, mustard, garlic, salt, red pepper, and black pepper. Cover and shake until combined; set aside.

**In a large saucepan** cook the zucchini and pea pods in lightly salted boiling water for 1 minute. Drain and place in a large bowl half-filled with ice water to cool. Drain well.

**In a large resealable plastic bag** place the zucchini, pea pods, sweet peppers, mushrooms, olives, and tomatoes. Pour marinade over vegetables. Seal bag. Turn bag to coat vegetables. Marinate in refrigerator for 1 to 4 hours, turning bag occasionally.

**To serve,** let stand at room temperature for 1 hour. Drain vegetables, discarding marinade. Arrange vegetables on a serving platter or in a bowl and serve with toothpicks. Makes 8 to 10 servings.

*Four-Cheese Spread*

## Chocolate Chai

*A steaming cup of tea is an age-old way to welcome folks in from the cold. Now, add a little kick to the tradition with spice and, if desired, a tipple of coffee liqueur. To spike the chocolate chai, stir in about 1 tablespoon coffee liqueur for each serving.*

  ⅔ cup sugar
  ½ cup unsweetened cocoa
     powder
  2 cups water
  8 chai-flavor tea bags
  4 cups milk
   Coffee liqueur (optional)

**In a large saucepan** stir together the sugar and cocoa powder. Stir in ½ cup of the water until smooth. Add the remaining water, whisking until combined. Heat to boiling; remove from heat. Add tea bags. Cover and steep for 20 minutes. Remove tea bags, squeezing out liquid from bags, and discard.

**Stir milk** and liqueur, if using, into chocolate mixture and heat just to simmering. Use a whisk to make the beverage frothy. Serve in mugs. Makes 8 (6-ounce) servings.

81

## Four-Cheese Spread

*Guests go wild for this dip—four luscious cheeses make it irresistibly oozy, while the egg mixture gives it a light, springy base.*

   Nonstick cooking spray
  ¾ cup shredded Gruyère cheese
    (3 ounces)
  1½ cups shredded cheddar cheese
    (6 ounces)
  1½ cups shredded smoked Gouda
    cheese (6 ounces)
  ¾ cup finely shredded Parmesan
    cheese (3 ounces)
  3 eggs, lightly beaten
  2 green onions, sliced
  ⅛ teaspoon garlic powder
   Assorted crackers or toasted
    baguette slices

**Lightly coat** a 9-inch pie plate with cooking spray. Place the Gruyère cheese in the pie plate. Layer with cheddar cheese, Gouda cheese, and Parmesan cheese; set aside.

**In a small bowl** whisk together the eggs, green onions, and garlic powder. Pour evenly over cheese in pie plate. Press down lightly with the back of a spoon.

**Bake, uncovered,** in a 325°F oven for 25 to 30 minutes or until mixture appears set. Serve immediately as a spread for crackers or baguette slices. Makes 8 to 10 servings.

**TO MAKE AHEAD:** Layer the cheeses in the pie plate and have the green onions sliced; cover and refrigerate. Before serving, whisk together the egg mixture and pour over the cheeses. Bake as above.

*Snack Mix Drops*

# Mini White Chocolate Cheesecakes

*End your caroling party on a high note. These luscious orange-sparked cheesecakes will be remembered long after the strains of holiday carols have faded. Pictured on page 79.*

- 12 chocolate wafer cookies
- 1 8-ounce package cream cheese, softened
- 1 3-ounce package cream cheese, softened
- 2/3 cup sugar
- 1 tablespoon all-purpose flour
- 2 egg yolks
- 3 tablespoons half-and-half or light cream
- 3 ounces white chocolate baking squares, chopped, or 1/2 cup white baking pieces
- 2 teaspoons finely shredded orange peel
- 2 tablespoons light-colored corn syrup
- 1 tablespoon water
- 1 tablespoon butter
- 1/2 cup semisweet chocolate pieces
  Whipped cream (optional)
- 1 recipe Chocolate Lace Musical Notes (optional)

**Line twelve** 2½-inch muffin cups with paper bake cups. Crush wafer cookies and divide evenly among cups. Set cups aside.

**For filling,** in a large mixing bowl beat cream cheese, sugar, and flour with an electric mixer until combined. Add egg yolks all at once, beating on low speed just until combined. Stir in half-and-half, chopped white chocolate, and orange peel. Divide filling among prepared muffin cups, being careful not to disturb the cookie crumbs.

**Bake in a 350°F oven** for 20 to 25 minutes or until cheesecakes appear set. Cool in pan on a wire rack for 5 minutes. Remove cheesecakes from pan and cool on wire racks for 1 hour. Arrange on a tray. Cover and chill

82

# Snack Mix Drops

*For a resounding refrain to the evening, send everyone home with a decorated gift box filled with these irresistible sweet-and-salty snacks. Of course, you'll want to set a few out on the serving buffet as a prelude to the gift.*

- 2 cups potato sticks (shoestring potatoes)
- 1/2 cup dried pineapple, chopped
- 1/2 cup smoked almonds, coarsely chopped
- 1/4 cup dried cranberries
- 6 ounces vanilla-flavored candy coating, chopped
- 1 tablespoon shortening

**Line a cookie sheet** with waxed paper; set aside. In a large bowl stir together potato sticks, pineapple, almonds, and cranberries; set aside.

**In a medium saucepan** melt candy coating and shortening over low heat. Pour coating mixture over fruit mixture; toss gently to coat.

**Quickly drop** mixture from teaspoons onto prepared cookie sheet. Let stand about 1 hour or until set. Makes about 24 pieces.

**TO MAKE AHEAD:** Place drops in layers separated by waxed paper in an airtight container. Cover. Store at room temperature up to 3 days. Do not freeze.

cheesecakes in the refrigerator at least 4 hours before serving.

**For topping,** in a small saucepan heat corn syrup, water, and butter until butter melts and mixture just boils. Pour over chocolate pieces in a small bowl; let stand 1 minute. Stir until smooth. Spoon over top of each cheesecake. Chill for 5 to 10 minutes or until chocolate is set. If desired, garnish with whipped cream and Chocolate Lace Musical Notes. Makes 12 servings.

**CHOCOLATE LACE MUSICAL NOTES:** In a small saucepan melt 1 ounce semisweet chocolate over low heat, stirring constantly. Let cool slightly. Place in a small heavy plastic bag. Cut a small hole in a corner; pipe musical note shapes onto waxed paper. Let garnishes stand in a cool, dry place until firm.

## white chocolate woes

From baking bars to baking pieces and white candy coating, it's difficult to determine one white chocolate product from another. What you need to know is this: Some products contain cocoa butter, while others do not. Only products having cocoa butter can truly be labeled "white chocolate." Read the recipe to find out exactly what product to buy. If the recipe specifies white chocolate, check the label ingredient listing for the words cocoa butter.

*Shrimp and Bacon
Triangle Puffs*

83

# Shrimp and Bacon Triangle Puffs

*A mix of bacon, shrimp, green onions, and carrots meld beautifully together in a flavorful cream-cheese base. Slather it between triangles of flaky puff pastry, and you'll really make a food lover's heart sing!*

1   17.3-ounce package frozen puff
     pastry (2 sheets), thawed
2   3-ounce packages cream
     cheese, softened
1   tablespoon Dijon-style mustard
1   tablespoon Worcestershire
     sauce for chicken
1   tablespoon thinly sliced green
     onion or snipped chives
2½  cups chopped, cooked, peeled,
     and deveined shrimp (about
     18 ounces uncooked)
⅓   cup shredded carrot
4   slices bacon, crisp-cooked, drained,
     and crumbled (⅓ cup)
     Shredded carrot (optional)

**Line 2 large baking sheets** with parchment paper; set aside. Unfold 1 sheet of puff pastry on a lightly floured surface. Using a pastry wheel or a sharp knife, cut sheet into 9 squares (about 3×3 inches each); cut each square diagonally in half to make a total of 18 triangles. Place triangles about 1 inch apart on prepared baking sheets.

**Bake in a 425°F oven** for 12 to 15 minutes or until golden. Remove from baking sheet and cool on a wire rack. Repeat with remaining sheet of puff pastry.

**For filling,** in a medium bowl combine cream cheese, mustard, Worcestershire sauce, and green onion. Fold in cooked shrimp, carrot, and bacon.

**To assemble,** using a small serrated knife, split each pastry triangle in half horizontally. Spread a tablespoon of filling on the bottom portion of each; replace top layer. If desired, cover and chill up to 2 hours before serving. If desired, serve on top of shredded carrot. Makes 36.

# extra touches

## INVITATION AND MENU

Guests will know the party's theme the minute the invitations arrive. The same materials make up a songbook-style menu for the buffet table.

▦ Invitations: Print out your invitation on scrapbooking vellum, centering the wording on a 4½x6-inch area and allowing for the ribbon at the top. See the photographs *below* for details. Cut music-theme scrapbooking paper to 5x6½ inches. Center the vellum over the print paper. Punch two holes in the top and tie ribbon through them to assemble the invitation. If desired, cut a strip of music-themed print vellum to fit over the wording; lay it over the top when joining all the layers.

▦ Menu Book: Print a title and menu pages on half sheets (5½x8½ inches) of plain vellum. Cut 6x9-inch pieces of music-print paper for the backs. Cut 5½x8½-inch pieces of music-patterned vellum for the covers. For each menu, center the menu page, title page, and cover over the back. Punch two pairs of holes through all layers and join them with knotted ribbons.

## TABLE TRICKS

Create an eye-catching table covering in a matter of minutes. Cut music notes from the patterns on *page 157* or use purchased die-cut shapes. Scatter the music notes over the cloth and runner. Cover it all with a sheer white curtain for softness.

## TREAT BOXES

▦ Send home Snack Mix Drops, *page 82,* or other treats in decorated boxes. Cover boxes and lids with decorative papers as if wrapping a package. Using the boxes pictured *below* and *opposite,* decorate the box tops with ribbons, punched or die-cut shapes, or woven strips of paper.

NOTE: Make sure all materials in contact with food are nontoxic.

〰 Spread notes of joy throughout the house with easy music-theme decorations and invitations.

## WELCOME NOTE

Greet guests with a treble clef wreath. Enlarge the pattern on *page 157* to scale and cut it from 1-inch-thick plastic foam using a serrated knife. Even the edges with fine sandpaper. Glue ribbon to the exposed sides. Hot-glue dried ferns to the front. Add berries and sheer ribbon for a final trim.

Raise Your Voice
in Song!

You are invited
to a
**Caroling
Party**
on December 7th
at 6 p.m. at
423 Polk Blvd.

*Afterwards,
we'll chase the chill
with hot spiked chai
and a harmonious
mix of sweet and
savory snacks!*

84

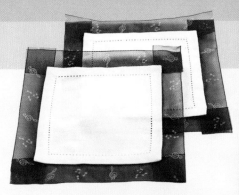

## NOTEWORTHY NAPKINS

▓ Give plain cocktail napkins a festive flair by adding ribbon trim. Cut sheer 1½-inch-wide ribbon to fit purchased napkins, letting the ribbons overlap at the corners. NOTE: To keep the ribbons from fraying, cut them with a wood-burning tool or run fabric glue along the cut edges. Using a stamp pad and small rubber stamps, stamp music motifs along the ribbons. Fuse the napkin over the ribbons using fusing tape.

## SERVING TRAY LACE

Decorate one or more layers of a tiered tray with custom-made doilies (see *page 78*). Cut 4-inch-wide strips of decorative paper and punch the edge with a lace punch.

See *photograph 1* for details. Fold the paper in half lengthwise 1¼ inches from the punched edge. Cut slashes to the fold line. Tape the trim around the plate so the lace edge hangs down and the slashed sections overlap. See *photograph 2* for details. Cut a circle to fit the center of the plate and the paper ends. Slash from the edge to the center and cut a circle to fit

around the plate tier. Lay the circle over the plate. See *photograph 2* for details.

## TRIM A TREE

Set up a coffee station, *above*, with a tiny music-trimmed tree. Using paper punches, cut tiny music symbols from decorative papers. Make garlands from scraps of the serving tray paper. Glue pieces of

paper back-to-back and cut narrow strips for the garland. Wrap the tree in the garlands and perch the notes on the branches. For the topper, fold a 28-inch length of 19-gauge wire in half and twist it together. Shape it using a die-cut or the pattern on *page 157*. Wrap the end wires around an alligator clip. See the photograph *above*. Brush the ornament with glue and sprinkle it with glitter.

# party cakes

*Deep Chocolate Cake with
Double-Malt Topping*

There's something about a big, beautiful cake that says "let's celebrate" better than any dessert around. In this selection of high-and-mighty beauties and short-and-sweet treats, you'll find just the right finale for any occasion.

## Deep Chocolate Cake with Double-Malt Topping

*Serving a house-full of kids and adults? This is your cake! Deeply flavored unsweetened chocolate makes it sophisticated enough for grown-up palates, while the malted milk balls make it fun for kids.*

½ cup unsweetened cocoa powder
2 cups all-purpose flour
1 teaspoon baking powder
½ teaspoon baking soda
⅔ cup butter, softened
1¾ cups sugar
3 eggs
4 ounces unsweetened chocolate, melted and cooled
2 teaspoons vanilla
1½ cups milk
1 recipe Chocolate Malt Frosting
2 cups malted milk balls or miniature malted milk balls

**Grease** three 8×8×2-inch square or 9×1½-inch-round cake pans. Lightly dust each pan with 1 teaspoon of the cocoa powder; set aside. In a medium bowl stir together the remaining cocoa powder, flour, baking powder, and baking soda; set aside.

**In a large mixing bowl** beat butter with an electric mixer on medium to high speed for 30 seconds. Add sugar; beat until combined. Add eggs, 1 at a time, beating for 30 seconds after each. Beat in cooled chocolate and vanilla. Alternately add flour mixture and milk to beaten mixture, beating on low speed until thoroughly combined. Divide batter evenly among the prepared pans; spread evenly.

**Bake in a 350°F oven** for 17 to 20 minutes or until a wooden toothpick inserted near the centers comes out clean. Cool cakes in pans on wire racks for 10 minutes. Remove cakes from pans. Cool thoroughly on wire racks.

**Prepare** Chocolate Malt Frosting.

**To assemble cake,** spread ¾ cup of the Chocolate Malt Frosting on tops of 2 of the layers and stack on a serving plate. Add top layer; frost the top and sides of the cake, reserving some frosting for the piping. Place the remaining frosting in a decorating bag fitted with a medium round tip. Starting from the bottom, pipe a zigzag pattern on sides and top edge of cake. If desired, coarsely chop or halve some of the malted milk balls. Decorate the cake with the malted milk balls. Cover and chill until ready to serve. Cover and store any leftovers in the refrigerator. Makes 20 servings.

**CHOCOLATE MALT FROSTING:**
In a medium saucepan bring 2 cups whipping cream just to boiling over medium-high heat. Remove from heat. Stir in ⅓ cup malt powder. Add two 11½-ounce packages milk chocolate pieces (do not stir). Cover and let stand for 5 minutes. Stir until smooth. (Mixture will be thin.) Transfer to a large mixing bowl. Cover and refrigerate about 3 hours or until frosting is thoroughly chilled. Set bowl of frosting in a larger bowl of ice water. Beat frosting with an electric mixer on medium speed about 3 minutes or until fluffy and of spreading consistency. (The frosting will turn a light brown color with beating.)

**TO MAKE AHEAD:** Prepare and bake cakes; cool completely. Place cake layers on baking sheets; freeze until firm. Once firm, place cakes in large freezer bags; seal, label, and freeze up to 3 months. To serve, thaw cake layers at room temperature for several hours. Frost as directed.

*Raspberry and White Chocolate Dacquoise*

# Raspberry and White Chocolate Dacquoise

¾ cup powdered sugar
1 tablespoon cornstarch
8 egg whites
¼ teaspoon cream of tartar
1 cup granulated sugar
8 ounces white chocolate baking squares with cocoa butter, chopped
2 cups whipping cream
¾ cup frozen unsweetened raspberries, thawed
4 ounces bittersweet or semisweet chocolate, chopped
½ cup whipping cream
1 tablespoon butter
¼ cup sliced almonds, toasted
Fresh raspberries

**To make meringue rectangles,** draw two 15×4½-inch rectangles on 1 sheet of parchment paper, leaving about 2 inches between rectangles, and one 15×4½-inch rectangle on another sheet of parchment paper. Place paper with marked sides down on 2 very large baking sheets; set aside.

**Sift together** powdered sugar and cornstarch; set aside. In a large mixing bowl place egg whites, cream of tartar, and ⅛ teaspoon salt. Let stand at room temperature for 30 minutes. Beat white mixture with electric mixer on medium speed until soft peaks form. Gradually beat in granulated sugar, beating on high speed until stiff peaks form (tips stand straight). Fold in powdered sugar mixture with a rubber spatula.

**Divide** meringue mixture evenly among traced rectangles on parchment paper, spreading to edges of rectangles. Bake both baking sheets at the same time, on 2 oven racks, in a 250°F oven for 1 hour. Reduce oven temperature to 200°F. Bake 2 hours more. Remove from oven; cool completely on pans on wire racks. Carefully peel meringues off parchment paper. Meringues can be wrapped in plastic wrap and stored at room temperature up to 24 hours.

**Meanwhile,** in a large bowl place white chocolate. In small saucepan heat 1 cup of the whipping cream just to boiling. Pour hot cream over white chocolate; do not stir. Let stand for 5 minutes. Whisk until chocolate is melted and smooth. Gradually stir in remaining 1 cup whipping cream until smooth. Cover and chill 2 hours or until completely cool. Place the ¾ cup thawed frozen raspberries in a blender or food processor. Cover and blend or process until smooth. Press through a fine-mesh sieve; discard seeds. You should have ¼ cup puree. Cover and chill puree until needed.

**Using an electric mixer,** beat chilled white chocolate mixture just until stiff peaks begin to form (do not overbeat). Remove half of the mixture (about 1½ cups) to a medium bowl; fold in raspberry puree. Cover and chill raspberry mixture and remaining white chocolate mixture for 4 to 24 hours.

**To assemble,** place 1 meringue on serving plate. Spread raspberry mixture over meringue. Top with second meringue and spread white chocolate mixture over meringue. Top with third meringue. Cover; chill for 2 to 24 hours.

**For ganache,** place bittersweet chocolate in a medium bowl. In a small saucepan heat the ½ cup whipping cream and butter just to boiling. Pour hot cream mixture over chocolate; do not stir. Let stand for 5 minutes; whisk until smooth. Chill for 10 minutes.

**Pour ganache** over top of chilled dacquoise, allowing some to run slightly over the edge of the top meringue. Garnish top with almonds and fresh raspberries. Cut with a serrated knife, running blade under hot water between cuts. Makes 12 to 14 servings.

# Glazed Gingerbread Cake

*Cakes baked in fluted tube pans are a baker's dream—they're pretty the minute they come out of the pan. Just add a glaze and ginger, and this one is set to impress.*

    3  cups all-purpose flour
 1½  teaspoons ground cinnamon
 1½  teaspoons ground ginger
    1  teaspoon baking powder
    1  teaspoon baking soda
    1  cup shortening
  ½  cup packed brown sugar
    2  eggs
    1  cup mild-flavored molasses
    1  cup water
    1  cup powdered sugar
    1  tablespoon lemon juice
  ¼  teaspoon vanilla
       Crystallized ginger strips
       (optional)

**Grease** a 10-inch fluted tube pan; set aside. In a large bowl stir together flour, cinnamon, ground ginger, baking powder, and baking soda; set aside.

**In a large mixing bowl** beat shortening with an electric mixer on medium speed for 30 seconds. Add brown sugar; beat until fluffy. Add eggs and molasses; beat for 1 minute. Alternately add flour mixture and water to egg mixture, beating on low speed after each addition until combined. Pour batter into prepared pan.

**Bake in a 350°F oven** for 45 to 50 minutes or until a wooden toothpick inserted near the center comes out clean. Cool cake in pan on a wire rack for 30 minutes. Remove cake from pan and cool completely.

**Meanwhile,** for glaze, in a small mixing bowl combine powdered sugar, lemon juice, and vanilla. If necessary, add additional lemon juice, 1 teaspoon at a time, until glaze is of drizzling consistency. Drizzle glaze over cake. If desired, garnish with crystallized ginger. Serves 12 to 16.

*Glazed Gingerbread Cake*

89

# Rosemary Pound Cake

*The most humble cakes often become all-time favorites for family gatherings.*

    2  cups sifted cake flour
    1  teaspoon baking powder
    1  cup butter, softened
    1  cup granulated sugar
  ¼  cup honey
    5  eggs
    1  tablespoon snipped fresh
       rosemary or 1 teaspoon dried
       rosemary, crushed
 1½  teaspoons orange flower water
       or ¼ teaspoon orange extract
 1¼  teaspoons finely shredded
       orange peel
 1½  teaspoons orange juice
    1  recipe Orange Juice Glaze

**Grease and flour** two 8×4×2-inch loaf pans; set aside. In a small bowl stir together cake flour and baking powder; set aside.

**In a large mixing bowl** beat butter and granulated sugar with an electric mixer on medium speed about 6 minutes or until light and creamy. Beat in honey. Add eggs, 1 at a time, beating for 1 minute after each. (Batter may look slightly curdled.) Gradually add flour mixture to the egg mixture, beating on low speed just until combined. Gently stir in snipped rosemary, orange flower water, orange peel, and orange juice. Divide batter between prepared pans.

**Bake in a 325°F oven** for 45 to 50 minutes or until a wooden toothpick inserted near the centers comes out clean. Cool in pans on wire racks for 10 minutes. Remove from pans; cool thoroughly on wire racks. Spread with Orange Juice Glaze. Makes 20 servings.

**ORANGE JUICE GLAZE:** In a small bowl stir together ⅔ cup powdered sugar and 1 tablespoon orange juice.

# Petite Caramel Apples and Pears

✳

*Charming lady apples also are known as pocket or lunch-box apples. If you can't find the petite fruit, substitute a favorite apple or pear variety and cut it into quarters for serving.*

8 to 10  small apples and/or pears, such as lady apples or Forelle or Seckel pears
½ cup butter
1 cup packed brown sugar
1 cup half-and-half or light cream
½ cup light-colored corn syrup
½ teaspoon vanilla

**Lightly grease** a large baking sheet; set aside. Wash fruit and pat dry. Insert a wooden skewer into the stem end of each piece of fruit; set aside.

**In a medium saucepan** melt butter over low heat. Add brown sugar, half-and-half, and corn syrup; mix well. Cook and stir over medium-high heat until mixture boils. Clip a candy thermometer to the side of the pan. Reduce heat to medium; continue boiling at a moderate, steady rate, stirring frequently, until the thermometer registers 248°F, firm-ball stage (25 to 30 minutes). Adjust heat as necessary to maintain a steady boil.

**Remove saucepan** from heat; remove thermometer. Stir in vanilla. Working quickly, dip each apple or pear into the hot caramel mixture, turning to coat about two-thirds of the fruit. Lift fruit out of caramel, twirling gently to let excess caramel run back into saucepan. Place coated fruit on prepared baking sheet. Cool. Remove skewers. Makes 8 to 10.

**NOTE:** If desired, drizzle any remaining caramel mixture around the edges and down the sides of the frosted cake. Or pour caramel into a shallow dish; refrigerate and reheat later for ice cream topping.

# Caramel Apple Cake

✳

*For Thanksgiving, if you're looking for something a little less predictable than pumpkin pie, try this apple-and-spice beauty. Serve with a knife and fork so guests can slice into the caramel apples and pears*

¼ cup butter
2 eggs
2 cups all-purpose flour
1½ teaspoons baking powder
1 teaspoon ground cinnamon
½ teaspoon baking soda
¼ teaspoon ground nutmeg
¼ teaspoon ground cloves
¼ teaspoon ground ginger
¼ cup shortening
1½ cups granulated sugar
½ teaspoon vanilla
¼ cup buttermilk or sour milk*
1 cup applesauce
1 recipe Butter Frosting
1 recipe Petite Caramel Apples and Pears

**Let butter and eggs stand** at room temperature for 30 minutes. Grease and lightly flour two 8×1½-inch round cake pans; set aside. In a medium bowl stir together the flour, baking powder, cinnamon, baking soda, nutmeg, cloves, and ginger; set aside.

**In a large mixing bowl** beat butter and shortening with an electric mixer on medium to high speed for 30 seconds. Add granulated sugar and vanilla; beat until well combined. Add eggs, 1 at a time, beating well after each. Stir together buttermilk and applesauce. Alternately add flour mixture and buttermilk to beaten mixture, beating on low speed after each addition just until combined. Divide batter between pans.

**Bake in a 350°F oven** about 35 minutes or until a wooden toothpick inserted near the centers comes out clean. Cool cakes in pans on wire racks for 10 minutes. Remove from pans. Cool thoroughly on wire racks. Prepare

Butter Frosting. Frost tops of layers with Butter Frosting. Stack cake layers. Arrange Petite Caramel Apples and Pears on and around cake. Serves 8 to 10.

**BUTTER FROSTING:** In a large mixing bowl beat ⅓ cup softened butter with an electric mixer on medium speed until fluffy. Gradually add 2 cups powdered sugar, beating well. Slowly beat in 2 tablespoons milk and 1 teaspoon vanilla. Slowly beat in 2½ cups powdered sugar. Beat in additional milk, if necessary, until frosting is of spreading consistency.

**\*NOTE:** To make sour milk, add enough milk to 1 teaspoon lemon juice to make ¼ cup. Let stand 5 minutes.

To dip apples or pears into caramel, insert a wooden or metal skewer near the stem of the fruit. Dip about two-thirds of the fruit into the caramel, then give it a twirl and let the excess caramel run back into the saucepan.

Place the partially coated fruit on a greased baking sheet; cool. Use a fork to steady the fruit as you remove the skewer.

90

*Caramel Apple Cake with Petite Caramel Apples and Pears*

*Festive Angel Cake*

**Separate eggs.** Let egg whites and egg yolks stand at room temperature for 30 minutes. Grease and lightly flour a 15×10×1-inch baking pan; set aside. In a small bowl stir together the flour, lemon peel, and baking powder; set aside.

**In a medium mixing bowl** beat egg yolks with an electric mixer on high speed for 5 minutes or until thick and lemon colored. Beat in the 2 tablespoons lemon juice until combined. Gradually add the ⅓ cup granulated sugar; beat on high speed until sugar is almost dissolved.

**Thoroughly wash beaters.** In a large mixing bowl beat egg whites on medium speed until soft peaks form (tips curl). Gradually add the ½ cup granulated sugar, beating until stiff peaks form (tips stand straight). Fold egg yolk mixture into beaten egg whites. Sprinkle flour mixture over egg mixture; fold gently until combined. Spread batter evenly in prepared pan. Sprinkle evenly with 1 cup almonds.

**Bake in a 375°F oven** for 12 to 15 minutes or until cake springs back when lightly touched. Immediately loosen edges of cake from pan; turn cake out onto towel sprinkled with sifted powdered sugar. Roll up towel and cake into a spiral starting from short side. Cool on wire rack.

**For filling,** in a medium bowl beat cream cheese with an electric mixer until fluffy. Beat in lemon curd until combined. In another bowl beat whipping cream with the electric mixer until soft peaks form. Fold into cream cheese mixture. Unroll cake; remove towel. Spread filling over cake to within 1 inch of edges. Roll up cake starting from a short side. If desired, cover and refrigerate cake up to 4 hours.

**If desired,** drizzle Lemon Icing over cake roll and sprinkle with additional toasted almonds. Makes 10 servings.

**LEMON ICING:** In a small bowl combine ¾ cup powdered sugar, ½ teaspoon finely shredded lemon peel, and 2 teaspoons lemon juice. Stir in additional lemon juice, 1 teaspoon at a time, until icing is of drizzling consistency.

## Festive Angel Cake

*Dreaming of a white Christmas? Make this dreamy all-white cake that's as light and wondrous as a Christmas Eve snowfall. (P.S. No one need know that all the magic starts with a mix.)*

 1  16-ounce package angel food cake mix
 4  cups powdered sugar
 ¼  cup hot water
    Crushed rock candy
    Lavender sprigs (optional)

**Prepare** angel food cake mix according to package directions. Cool as directed.

**For icing,** combine powdered sugar and hot water; if necessary, stir in additional water, 1 teaspoon at a time, to make desired consistency. Spread icing over cake. Sprinkle crushed rock candy over top of cake. If desired, garnish bottom edge of cake with lavender sprigs. Makes 12 servings.

## Lemon-Almond Cake Roll

*Reminiscent of a classic Victorian jelly-roll and just as old-fashioned, this cake brings a touch of yesteryear's charm to the table.*

 4  eggs
 ½  cup all-purpose flour
 2  teaspoons finely shredded lemon peel
 1  teaspoon baking powder
 2  tablespoons lemon juice
 ⅓  cup granulated sugar
 ½  cup granulated sugar
 1  cup chopped almonds, toasted
    Powdered sugar
 1  3-ounce package cream cheese, softened
 ¼  cup purchased lemon curd
 ½  cup whipping cream
 1  recipe Lemon Icing (optional)
    Chopped almonds, toasted (optional)

92

# Baumkuchen

*This is the sort of rare and wonderful treat you rarely find outside of a European pastry shop. Pronounced bowm-KYOO-kin, the name roughly translates as "tree cake." When sliced, the layers resemble rings on a crosscut tree.*

- 10 eggs
- 1 cup all-purpose flour
- ½ cup cornstarch
- ¼ teaspoon salt
- ¾ cup butter, softened
- ¾ cup granulated sugar
- 2 teaspoons finely shredded lemon peel
- 1 teaspoon vanilla
- ¼ cup granulated sugar
- 1 recipe Vanilla Glaze
- 1 recipe Chocolate Glaze
  Fresh mint sprigs (optional)
  Fresh raspberries (optional)

**Separate eggs.** Let egg whites and egg yolks stand at room temperature for 30 minutes. Grease an 8-inch springform pan; set aside. In a small bowl stir together the flour, cornstarch, and salt; set aside.

**In a medium mixing bowl** beat egg yolks with an electric mixer on high speed for 5 minutes or until thick and lemon colored; set aside. In an extra large mixing bowl beat butter with an electric mixer on medium to high speed for 30 seconds. Gradually add the ¾ cup granulated sugar, lemon peel, and vanilla. Add egg yolks, beating well. Stir flour mixture into butter mixture.

**Thoroughly wash beaters.** In a large mixing bowl beat egg whites on medium speed until soft peaks form (tips curl). Gradually add the ¼ cup granulated sugar, beating on high speed until stiff peaks form (tips stand straight). Fold egg white mixture into egg yolk mixture.

**Spread** ⅓ cup of the batter evenly in the bottom of the prepared pan. Place under broiler 5 inches from heat; broil

Baumkuchen

for 1 to 2 minutes or until lightly browned. (Give pan a half-turn for even browning, if needed.) Do not overbrown. Remove from broiler. Spread another ⅓ cup batter on top of first layer. Broil as before, turning, if necessary. Repeat, making 15 to 17 layers in all. Cool 10 minutes. Loosen cake and remove sides of pan; cool completely on a wire rack.

**Cut into 12 wedges.** Place wedges on wire rack with waxed paper beneath. Spread Vanilla Glaze over 6 wedges and spread Chocolate Glaze over remaining 6 wedges, covering tops and letting some glaze drip down the sides. Drizzle vanilla-glazed wedges with Chocolate Glaze and drizzle chocolate-glazed

wedges with Vanilla Glaze. Let dry. If desired, garnish with mint sprigs and raspberries. Makes 12 servings.

**VANILLA GLAZE:** Combine 2 cups powdered sugar and 1 teaspoon vanilla. Add enough milk (2 to 3 tablespoons) until glaze is of spooning consistency.

**CHOCOLATE GLAZE:** In a small saucepan melt 1½ ounces unsweetened chocolate and 2 tablespoons butter over low heat, stirring constantly; remove from heat. Stir in 1½ cups powdered sugar and 1 teaspoon vanilla until crumbly. Add enough boiling water (2 to 3 tablespoons) to make a thin glaze.

# a holiday
# wine tasting

*Blue Cheese-Ricotta Dip,*
*page 102*

Host a new kind of holiday open house—a festive wine tasting featuring five lesser-known wines guests will enjoy getting to know. Serve them alongside flavorful foods that help bring out all that's wonderful about your new finds.

Chardonnay, White Zinfandel, Merlot, and Cabernet Sauvignon—many casual wine drinkers have settled on one of these as their "usual." Indeed they're the top-selling wines in America.

And yet, as anyone who's ever explored a wine shop knows, there's a whole world of wonderful wines out there waiting to be discovered. Where to begin?

Here's a great way to expand your world when it comes to wine: Invite friends over to try five lesser-known wines; selections that are sure to turn heads and get conversations going.

This party features five different wines (Shiraz, rosé, Riesling, Prosecco, and Pinot Noir) matched with foods that go beautifully with each. Set up five wine-tasting stations (a great way to get guests to mingle) and showcase one wine and the food that goes with it at each station.

You'll also find some fun ideas for decorations and party favors. A wine placard describing each wine lets guests learn a little more about what they're tasting (copy the text from the following green sidebars, if you wish). Guests will appreciate business-size cards with the names of the specific wines printed on each; on the back, they can write tasting notes, if they wish. Matching stands make the cards easy to spot and personalized holders are the perfect take-home gift. The cards will serve your friends as a reminder when they're at the wine shop trying to remember that marvelous wine they tasted at your house.

*Artichoke Caponata, page 99*

How to select specific wines for each type you're showcasing? Those on the following pages are a few widely available selections. Or, perhaps now's the time to get to know your local wine merchant—most love to talk about wine. Let him or her know what you're up to, what varieties you're looking for, and what you wish to spend; chances are, they'll point you in interesting directions.

There are no hard-and-fast rules here; if you wish, you can focus on just one or two of the wines, and offer several examples of each. You'll also find "no cook" options for foods to go with all the wines, so you can mix and match homemade appetizers with high-quality purchased items that will save you time.

Keep it easygoing, accessible, and fun. The idea is simply this: Here are some wines you'll love getting to know; here are some foods that bring out the best in them. Enjoy!

*Roquefort-Walnut Stuffed Mushrooms*

*Maple-Dijon Salmon Bites*

96

# Maple-Dijon Salmon Bites

*The rich, distinct flavors in these little bites beg for a food-friendly Pinot Noir. Gallo of Sonoma's Pinot Noir offers bright red-fruit flavors that bring up the tarts' maple-tinged sweetness.*

    3 tablespoons finely chopped
      hazelnuts (filberts) or almonds
    1 tablespoon butter
    4 ounces smoked salmon (not
      lox), flaked, with skin and
      bones removed
    1 2.1-ounce package (15) baked
      miniature phyllo dough shells
    2 tablespoons pure maple syrup
    2 tablespoons Dijon-style mustard
    1 teaspoon snipped fresh thyme,
      or ¼ teaspoon dried thyme,
      crushed

**In a small skillet** cook and stir nuts in butter over medium heat for 3 to 4 minutes or until toasted; set aside.

**Evenly divide** salmon flakes among phyllo shells. In a small bowl stir together the maple syrup, mustard, and thyme. Drizzle mixture evenly over salmon (about 1 teaspoon per shell). Top with nuts. Makes 15 appetizers.

# Roquefort-Walnut Stuffed Mushrooms

*Walnuts and mushrooms are popular ingredients in Burgundy, France, so it figures they pair well with wines made from Pinot Noir, the "Noble grape of Burgundy." True Burgundies—from Burgundy, France—can be pricey, however, there are good exceptions.*

   24 large fresh mushrooms (1½ to
      2 inches in diameter)
    4 slices bacon
    ¼ cup sliced green onions (2)
    1 clove garlic, minced
    ⅔ cup fine dry bread crumbs

    ½ cup crumbled Roquefort or
      other blue cheese, such as
      Maytag or Point Reyes
      (2 ounces)
    ¼ cup chopped walnuts, toasted
    ¼ cup whipping cream

**Rinse** and drain mushrooms. Remove stems; reserve caps. Chop enough stems to make 1 cup; discard any remaining stems.

**In a large skillet cook** bacon over medium heat until crisp, turning once; remove bacon from skillet, reserving drippings in skillet. Crumble bacon and set aside. Cook 1 cup chopped stems, green onions, and garlic in the bacon drippings until tender. Remove from heat.

**Stir in bread crumbs,** cheese, walnuts, whipping cream, and reserved crumbled bacon. Spoon cheese mixture into mushroom caps. Arrange stuffed mushrooms in a 15×10×1-inch baking pan. Bake in a 425°F oven for 8 to 10 minutes or until heated through. Makes 24 mushrooms.

# extra touches

Make it easy for your guests to make note of their favorite wines. Business cards preprinted with the wine's name and basic information are displayed at each tasting station. On the back of each card is room for the taster's personal notes and comments.

Help guests keep track of their notes by providing little metal boxes to hold their cards. The plain containers are embellished with scrapbooking papers and trims and snippets of ribbon. Use the examples shown *below* for inspiration or personalize them even further. They're sure to be used and appreciated long after the party is over.

## WINE CARD HOLDERS
Purchase hinged metal boxes or plain business card holders in a neutral color.

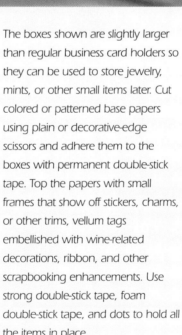

The boxes shown are slightly larger than regular business card holders so they can be used to store jewelry, mints, or other small items later. Cut colored or patterned base papers using plain or decorative-edge scissors and adhere them to the boxes with permanent double-stick tape. Top the papers with small frames that show off stickers, charms, or other trims, vellum tags embellished with wine-related decorations, ribbon, and other scrapbooking enhancements. Use strong double-stick tape, foam double-stick tape, and dots to hold all the items in place.

## WINE NOTE CARDS
Purchase blank business cards that have a decorative border from business or stationary stores. Abbreviate the information from the wine placards (so it fits onto the cards), then print it out on a home computer. The business card package will have details on how to make the copy work with your computer software. See the information included in this story for basics on each wine. Turn over the papers and print "Tasting Notes" and a series of lines on the back. Carefully tear the cards apart along the perforations.

*above*. Spiral the remaining wire outward. Make a loop and hang a bead at the end. See *page 96* for details.

## WINE STATION PLACARDS

■ Give your guests basic facts on the wines you serve by placing a framed information card at each station. Using a home computer, type out the wine description on decorative paper leaving at least a 1-inch margin on each side. Trim off the margin. Mount the description on vellum, leaving a ½-inch margin on each side. Mount the vellum on background paper so ½ inch shows on all sides. Add wine-related stickers or embellishments from the scrapbooking

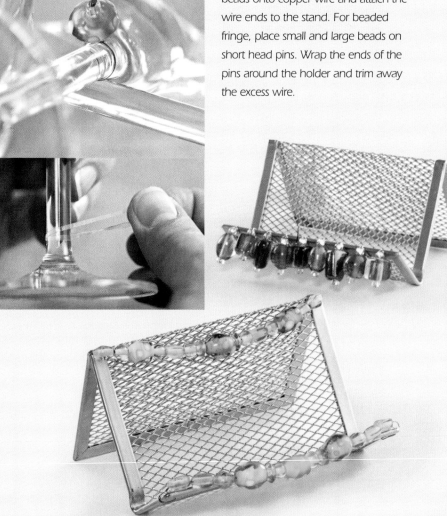

ROSÉ

*Description*

Rosé wines are commonly thought of as sweet; however, while most possess pleasant fruit flavors, many styles are dry and off-dry. Rosés get their pink hue because the skins of the grapes do not ferment with the juice as long as they do for reds. Because rosé can be made of many kinds of red grapes (such as Syrah, Pinot Noir, Grenache, and Cinsault), there are many styles of rosés available.

*At Table*

Serve crisp, dry styles of rosés as an apéritif with appetizers. Most pair well with spicy foods. Also remember them around the holidays—many pair well with turkey and traditional trimmings such as cranberry sauce and sweet potatoes. Serve chilled.

store and place the card in a simple frame. (The frames shown in this story measure 6×6 inches.)

## WINE CARD STANDS

■ Add beads to plain business card holders to draw attention to the wine cards. To add beaded strands, string beads onto copper wire and attach the wire ends to the stand. For beaded fringe, place small and large beads on short head pins. Wrap the ends of the pins around the holder and trim away the excess wire.

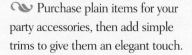

Purchase plain items for your party accessories, then add simple trims to give them an elegant touch.

## WINE GLASS CHARMS

■ Curlicue Charms: Using needlenose pliers, slip a spiral-style paper clip around the stem of the wine glass so it fits tightly against the bowl (see the photograph *above* for details). To hold the paper clip in place, wrap a small, clear rubber band around the stem two times and slide it to the top of the stem. See the photograph *right* for details. Hang S-shape paper clips (available at scrapbooking stores) from the spiral clip. ■ Beaded Stemware: Place one small and one medium bead on a head pin. Wrap the pin wire around the stem at the base of the bowl. See the photograph *above right* for details. Twist the wire back on itself just under the bead and trim the end. Add a rubber band as described *above*. ■ Dangling Beads: Tightly wrap the end of a 3-inch piece of silver wire around the stem just below the bowl; hold it in place with a rubber band as described

## pinot noir

Description: Pinot Noir (PEA-noh NWAR) is often called the "noble grape of Burgundy," as this is the grape from which Burgundy's plush red wines are made. Lighter bodied than Merlot and Cabernet, Pinot Noir wines generally offer the aromas and flavors of bright red fruits and are often described as soft, smooth, and elegant.

In a word: Silky.

At Table: Pairing equally well with meat, fish, and game, this is pretty much an all-purpose "never let you down" wine when it comes to food. Its versatility makes it a great choice to bring to a party when you don't know what will be served for dinner.

No-Cook Option: Look for Epoisse cheese at a specialty cheese shop. This strong cheese is made in Burgundy, where France's famous Pinot Noir wines are made.

Recommended: If you'd like to try a typical Burgundy from France, go with Louis Jadot Pinot Noir Bourgogne. From California, Gallo of Sonoma Pinot Noir offers a classic expression of this varietal. A reliable budget choice is Rex Goliath Pinot Noir.

# Artichoke Caponata

*Because they can be acidic, artichokes can be tough to pair with wine. A dry rosé brings down the sharpness of their acidity—an example of how wine makes food taste better. Pictured on page 95.*

- 3 13¾-ounce cans artichoke bottoms or 14-ounce cans artichoke hearts, drained and chopped
- ¼ cup olive oil
- 1 cup chopped onion (1 large)
- ½ cup chopped celery
- 2 cloves garlic, minced
- 1 14½-ounce can diced tomatoes
- ½ cup slivered pitted kalamata olives
- ⅓ cup white wine vinegar
- 2 tablespoons capers, drained
- 1 tablespoon sugar
- 1 teaspoon salt
- ¼ cup pine nuts, toasted
- ¼ cup coarsely snipped fresh basil
  Sliced baguette-style French bread or crackers
  Shaved dry Jack cheese or Parmesan cheese (optional)

**In a large skillet** cook artichokes in 3 tablespoons of the oil over medium-high heat about 8 minutes or until golden, stirring frequently. Remove artichokes; set aside. In same skillet cook onion and celery in remaining oil until tender. Stir in garlic. Cook and stir for 1 minute. Return artichokes to skillet.

**Add undrained tomatoes,** olives, vinegar, capers, sugar, and salt to skillet. Bring to a simmer over medium-high heat; reduce heat to low. Simmer, uncovered, for 10 to 15 minutes or until liquid is evaporated, stirring occasionally. Cool. Stir in pine nuts and basil. Transfer to a bowl; cover and chill for 2 hours or overnight.

**To serve,** let caponata stand at room temperature for 30 minutes before serving. Serve on slices of French bread or crackers. If desired, top with shaved cheese. Makes about 30 servings.

# Shrimp Crostini with Chimichurri Sauce

*Robert Hall Rosé de Robles brought some real attitude to this dish, bringing out the punchy flavors of the chimichurri sauce. You may want to serve this on individual plates with knives and forks as they can be a substantial starter for a dinner party.*

- 1 19-ounce can white kidney beans (cannellini), rinsed and drained
- 2 tablespoons olive oil
- ½ teaspoon salt
- ½ teaspoon ground black pepper
- 1 12-ounce loaf baguette-style French bread, bias-sliced into 24 slices
  Olive oil
- 24 fresh or frozen peeled, deveined large or jumbo shrimp, thawed
- 3 cloves garlic, minced
- 2 tablespoons butter
- 2 tablespoons dry white wine
- 1 recipe Chimichurri Sauce

**In food processor\*** combine beans, 2 tablespoons olive oil, salt, and pepper. Cover and process until smooth; set aside.

**For crostini,** lightly brush baguette slices with olive oil. Arrange in a single layer on baking sheets. Bake in a 425°F oven about 10 minutes or until lightly toasted. Cool on wire racks. Spread evenly with bean puree; set aside.

**To butterfly** the shrimp, make a small lengthwise slit down the back, cutting to but not through the opposite edge. In a large skillet cook garlic in 1 tablespoon of hot butter for 30 seconds. Add the shrimp. Cook for 2 to 4 minutes or until shrimp turn opaque, stirring frequently. Remove shrimp from skillet. Carefully add remaining 1 tablespoon butter and the wine to the skillet. Cook and stir to loosen any browned bits. Remove from heat. Return shrimp to skillet, tossing to coat.

**Place** 1 shrimp on each crostini so shrimp sits vertically on its back. Place on serving plates. Pool a little chimichurri sauce on plate around crostini. Makes 24 appetizers.

**CHIMICHURRI SAUCE:** In a food processor or blender combine 1 cup firmly packed fresh Italian (flat-leaf) parsley; ¼ cup olive oil; 2 tablespoons cider vinegar; 2 teaspoons snipped fresh thyme; 1 teaspoon paprika; 1 teaspoon bottled hot pepper sauce; 2 cloves garlic, coarsely chopped; ½ teaspoon salt; and ¼ teaspoon crushed red pepper. Cover and process or blend until smooth. If desired, season to taste with additional bottled hot pepper sauce.

**\*NOTE:** If you do not have a food processor, mash bean mixture with a potato masher or fork until nearly smooth.

99

*Chicken Drummettes with Plum Sauce*

## nonalcoholic options

All of the appetizers in this story are festive party foods that will be the highlight of any holiday occasion. If you're hosting a wine-tasting party, be sure to offer fun and enticing nonalcoholic beverage options for designated drivers and others who choose not to drink alcohol. For holiday-hued sparkle, add a dash of cranberry juice and a sprig of mint to seltzer on ice. Spear fresh cranberries and lime wedges with cocktail picks and drop into a frosted glass of bubbling club soda. Also look for nonalcoholic sparkling wines or fancy sodas such as Lorina's Sparkling Pink Lemonade and Sparkling Orangeade imported from France.

# Chicken Drummettes with Plum Sauce

*R.H. Phillips Shiraz is an easy-to-find choice to serve with these sweet and savory treats. The deep, fruity wine brings forward the plum and ginger notes in this classy take on drummies.*

    ¾  cup bottled plum sauce
    ¼  cup honey
    ¼  cup red wine vinegar
    1  tablespoon toasted sesame
       seeds*
    1  tablespoon grated fresh ginger
    2  cloves garlic, minced
   36  chicken wings (6 to 8 pounds)
1 to 1¼ teaspoons five-spice powder
    1  teaspoon salt
    ½  teaspoon ground black pepper
    2  tablespoons olive oil
       Blanched snow pea pods
       (optional)

**For sauce,** in a small saucepan combine plum sauce, honey, vinegar, sesame seeds, ginger, and garlic. Bring to boiling over medium heat, stirring occasionally. Reduce heat and cook, uncovered, for 3 minutes to blend flavors. Remove from heat; set aside.

**Trim wing tips** and middle flat part of each wing from meaty drummette portion. Discard tips and middles or reserve them for another use, such as making chicken stock. If desired, loosen meat from bony end of each drummette and push meat to other end of bone, leaving bare bone to serve as a handle. Spread the chicken drummettes in an even layer in a 15×10×1-inch baking pan.

**In a small bowl** combine five-spice powder, salt, and pepper. Sprinkle over drummettes in pan. Heat oil in a 12-inch nonstick skillet over medium heat. Add half the drummettes to hot skillet; cook about 10 minutes or until browned, turning occasionally to brown all sides. Return drummettes to the baking pan. Repeat with remaining chicken drummettes.

**Drizzle** ⅔ cup of the sauce over drummettes. Bake, uncovered, in a 400°F oven for 15 to 20 minutes or until chicken is no longer pink. Reheat remaining sauce and serve with hot drummettes. If desired, garnish serving dish with snow pea pods. Makes 36 drummettes.

**\*Note:** To toast sesame seeds, place in a dry skillet over medium heat. Shake skillet occasionally until seeds are golden. Remove from heat.

## dry crisp rosé

Description: Rosé wines are commonly thought of as sweet; however, while most rosés possess pleasant fruit flavors, many styles are dry and off-dry. Most rosés get their pink hue because the juice of the grapes do not ferment with their skins as long as they do for reds. Because rosé can be made of many kinds of red grapes (such as Syrah, Pinot Noir, Grenache, and Cinsault), there are many styles of rosés available.

In a word: Vibrant.

At Table: Serve crisp, dry styles of rosés as an apéritif with appetizers. Most pair well with spicy foods. Also remember them around the holidays—many pair well with turkey and traditional trimmings such as cranberry sauce and sweet potatoes. Serve chilled.

No-Cook Option: Try a jar of marinated artichokes and/or asparagus—these veggies are a challenge to pair with other wines but work well with dry rosé.

Recommended Rosés: To prove once and for all that pink isn't necessarily sweet, try the lush, bone-dry Château d'Aquéria Tavel from France. For a party-perfect sipper, bright and refreshing Solo Rosa Rosé is a winner. Also try Robert Hall Rosé de Robles, with zippy red-fruit and tangerine aromas.

## Lamb Pita Chips with Garlic-Yogurt Sauce

✳

*Some Syrahs offer just a hint of peppery flavor; the spicy notes of these chips really brings it out.*

- 4 large pita bread rounds
- ⅓ cup olive oil
  Salt
  Freshly ground black pepper
- 8 ounces lean ground lamb
- 4 ounces lean ground beef

- 2 tablespoons finely chopped onion
- ¼ cup coarsely chopped bottled roasted red sweet peppers
- 3 tablespoons snipped fresh parsley
- ½ teaspoon salt
- ¼ teaspoon ground coriander
- ¼ teaspoon freshly ground black pepper
- ⅛ teaspoon ground cumin
- 1 8-ounce carton plain yogurt
- 2 teaspoons Roasted Garlic Paste
  Slivered kalamata olives (optional)

**To make pita chips,** cut pita rounds in half crosswise. Split each in half horizontally (16 halves). Brush cut sides evenly with oil; sprinkle lightly with salt and black pepper. Cut each half into 3 wedges (48 wedges). Arrange wedges in a single layer on 2 large baking sheets. Bake in a 375°F oven about 12 minutes or until edges are golden brown and crisp. Set chips aside (may be made up to a day ahead).

**In a medium skillet** cook lamb, beef, and onion over medium heat until meat is brown and onion is tender; drain off fat. Stir in sweet peppers, parsley, ½ teaspoon salt, coriander, ¼ teaspoon pepper, and cumin. Heat through.

**In a small bowl** combine yogurt and Roasted Garlic Paste. To serve, spoon lamb mixture evenly onto each pita chip. Drizzle yogurt sauce over top. If desired, top with a few olive slivers. Makes 48 appetizers.

**ROASTED GARLIC PASTE:** To roast garlic, peel away the outer layers of skin from 1 head of garlic, leaving skins and cloves intact. Cut off the top ¼ inch, leaving the bulb intact but exposing the individual cloves. Place the garlic head, cut side up, in a custard cup. Drizzle with 2 teaspoons olive oil. Cover with foil and bake in a 425°F oven for 25 to 35 minutes or until the cloves feel soft when pressed. When cool enough to

handle, squeeze garlic from individual cloves. Mash garlic into a paste with a fork. Cover; refrigerate any remaining paste for another use up to 1 week.

## shiraz / syrah

Description: Syrah came to prominence in France's Rhone Valley but is now the most widely planted grape in Australia (where it is known as Shiraz). While there are many styles of Syrah available, most are full-bodied, dark-colored wines with vivid plum and black fruit flavors; they often exhibit spicy and smoky tones.

In a word: Exotic.

At Table: Great with roasts, braises, and other meaty, full-flavored dishes, and a shoo-in with barbecue.

No-Cook Option: Serve with a sharp cheese such as Parmigiano-Reggiano or Pecorino Romano.

Recommended Shiraz: Try California's R.H. Phillips Shiraz for bright, jammy raspberry flavors with nuances of oak and spice. From Southeastern Australia comes Wyndham Estate Bin 555 Shiraz, a rich and fruity choice, especially for the price. Chateau Ste. Michelle Columbia Valley Syrah is a luscious pick from Washington State.

101

*Lamb Pita Chips with Garlic-Yogurt Sauce*

Cut down on the last-minute holiday crunch by stocking up on wines that will see you through all the events of the season. With a few bottles of these, you'll be set.

Champagne and Sparkling Wines: As a hostess gift, for kicking off a holiday feast, and of course, for New Year's Eve, sparkling wines can't be beat. They're also wonderful companions for food—and they're one of the few wines that won't let you down when serving eggs (remember them for brunch). When serving a sparkling wine with food, try one labeled brut (which means it is dry); save the sweeter ones for apéritifs or dessert. Real Champagne—from the Champagne region in France—is expensive; try high-quality sparkling wines from California, such as Chandon Riche Extra Dry, Sofia Blanc de Blancs, and Domaine Carneros Brut by Taittinger. For budget picks, try a cava from Spain or Prosecco from Italy.

A Surefire White: Sure, Chardonnay is a crowd-pleaser, but to veer off that beaten path, try some less-familiar whites. For your party sipper, offer a Viognier; it's a fascinating wine—floral and fruity, with essences of peach, apricot, and pear. An elegant choice is Clay Station Viognier. Riesling is a shoo-in with turkey (see selections *right*). Light, crisp, and palate-clearing, Sauvignon Blanc works especially well for the long lunches and early dinners of New Year's Day. Try those from St. Supery and Geyser Peak Winery.

A No-Fail Red: Pinot Noir goes with just about anything; see selections on *page 99*. For something more full-bodied, stock up on Shiraz (see selections on *page 101*). Another great choice is Beaujolais; it's light and dry with fresh, fruity flavors. Choose more recent vintages and serve slightly chilled. Try Louis Jadot Beaujolais from France.

102

# Santa Fe Spiced Nuts

*Riesling packs enough flavor on its own to stand up to some spice. Trimbach Riesling, an elegant, fruity, and dry wine from Alsace, won't let you down with these kicky nuts.*

> Nonstick cooking spray
> 1 egg white
> 1 tablespoon frozen orange juice concentrate, thawed
> ¼ cup sugar
> 1 tablespoon chili powder
> 1 teaspoon garlic powder
> ½ teaspoon ground cumin
> ¼ teaspoon ground black pepper
> ¼ to ½ teaspoon cayenne pepper
> ¼ teaspoon celery salt
> ¼ teaspoon ground cinnamon
> 3 cups peanuts or mixed nuts

**Line** a 15×10×1-inch baking pan with foil. Coat foil with nonstick cooking spray; set aside. In a large bowl combine egg white, orange juice concentrate, sugar, chili powder, garlic powder, cumin, black pepper, cayenne pepper, celery salt, and cinnamon. Stir in nuts; toss to coat. Spread nuts in prepared baking pan. Bake in a 325°F oven for 20 minutes, stirring twice. Cool; break apart large clusters. Store in airtight container at room temperature up to 1 week. Makes 3 cups.

# Blue Cheese-Ricotta Dip

*Dry Rieslings pair beautifully with rich foods—and this dip is definitely rich! We enjoyed it with Lake Chalice Marlborough Riesling, a dry, crisp wine with a slightly floral accent. Pictured on page 94.*

> 1 15-ounce container ricotta cheese
> 8 ounces blue cheese, such as Gorgonzola or Maytag, crumbled (2 cups)

## dry reislings

**Description:** Riesling sometimes gets a reputation for being a real sweetie pie; indeed, many are on the sweeter side. However, some Rieslings, especially those from Alsace, can be quite dry. Often exhibiting refined peach and citrus flavors and floral aromas, Riesling has a vivid acidity that also gives it a refreshing crispness. Some display pleasant minerally undertones.

**In a word:** Elegant.

**At Table:** Try a dry, crisp Riesling as a party sipper in place of Chardonnay or Pinot Grigio. Riesling's hallmark acidity can pierce through rich foods, such as duck, pâté, and cream-sauced dishes. Riesling's vivid flavors also stand aup to spicy foods. Serve chilled.

**No-Cook Option:** Try it with purchased spiced nuts. For a cheese option, try a true Munster, a rich, strongly flavored cheese from Alsace.

**Recommended Rieslings:** To get to know a dry, elegant side of Riesling, choose those from the Alsace region of France—those from renowned wine-makers Hugel and Trimbach. From Australia, but similar in style, is Lake Chalice Marlborough Riesling, a crisp, dry wine with a slightly floral accent.

> 2 tablespoons apple cider or milk
> Freshly ground black pepper
> Snipped fresh chives or your favorite herb
> Green and/or red apple slices or crackers

**Allow ricotta** and blue cheese to stand at room temperature for 1 hour.

**In a medium bowl** stir together the ricotta and blue cheese, mashing with a fork until well combined. Stir in the apple cider. Add pepper to taste. Spoon into a serving bowl. Sprinkle with chives. Serve with apple slices or crackers. Makes 8 servings.

*Lemony Nut Madeleines*

103

# Lemony Nut Madeleines

*Pairing these with Zardetto Prosecco offers a great crash-course in how the flavors of food affect the flavors in wine—and vice versa. The Prosecco highlights the lemony flavor in the cookies, while the zing of the cookies make the sweet-tinged Prosecco seem just a little bit dryer.*

2 tablespoons butter, melted
2 tablespoons all-purpose flour
½ cup granulated sugar
2 egg yolks
½ cup butter, melted and cooled
½ teaspoon finely shredded lemon peel (set aside)
1 tablespoon lemon juice
½ teaspoon vanilla
½ cup all-purpose flour
½ teaspoon baking powder
⅛ teaspoon baking soda
⅛ teaspoon salt

¼ cup finely chopped almonds, toasted
2 egg whites, slightly beaten
Powdered sugar

**In a small bowl** stir together the 2 tablespoons melted butter and the 2 tablespoons flour. Coat twenty-four 3-inch madeleine molds with the butter-flour mixture. Set aside.

**In a medium mixing bowl** beat granulated sugar and egg yolks with an electric mixer on medium to high speed for 30 seconds. Add the ½ cup butter, lemon juice, and vanilla. Beat on low speed until combined; set aside.

**In a small bowl** stir together ½ cup flour, baking powder, baking soda, and salt. Sprinkle flour mixture over the egg

yolk mixture; gently fold in. Fold in almonds and lemon peel. Gently stir in egg whites. Spoon batter into prepared molds, filling each about half full (about 1 rounded tablespoon each).

**Bake in a 375°F oven** for 10 to 12 minutes or until edges are golden and tops spring back when lightly touched. Cool in molds for 1 minute. Using the point of a knife, loosen cookies from molds; invert onto a wire rack. Remove molds and cool cookies completely on a wire rack.

**Cover tightly** and store at room temperature up to 3 days. To serve, sift powdered sugar over cookies. Makes 24 madeleines.

# Christmastime

*Mitten Cookies*

# is cookie time

Plenty of magical things happen around the holidays, and one of the best is when eggs, flour, butter, and sugar—plus a few flourishes like chocolate, nuts, jam, and spices—morph into a beautiful array of gorgeous cookies. These seven great recipes help make the magic happen.

## Mitten Cookies

*Royal Icing makes a smooth, glossy coating for sugar-cookie cutouts. You can find meringue powder for the icing wherever cake decorating supplies are sold. If you don't have a mitten cookie cutter, make a pattern on a thin piece of cardboard: Trace around a child's hand, cut out the pattern, place the pattern on rolled out cookie dough, and cut around the pattern for each cookie.*

- ¼ cup butter, softened
- ¼ cup shortening
- 1 cup granulated sugar
- 1 teaspoon baking powder
- ¼ teaspoon baking soda
- ⅛ to ¼ teaspoon ground nutmeg
- ½ cup dairy sour cream
- 1 egg
- 1 teaspoon vanilla
- 2⅔ cups all-purpose flour
- 1 recipe Royal Icing (optional)
  Gumdrops, sliced (optional)

**In a large mixing bowl** beat butter and shortening with an electric mixer on medium to high speed for 30 seconds. Add granulated sugar, baking powder, baking soda, and nutmeg. Beat until combined, scraping sides of bowl occasionally. Beat in sour cream, egg, and vanilla until combined. Beat in as much of the flour as you can with the mixer. Stir in any remaining flour with a wooden spoon. Divide dough in half. Cover; chill about 2 hours or until easy to handle.

**On a lightly floured surface,** roll dough, half at a time, until ¼ inch thick. Using a 2½-inch mitten cookie cutter, cut out cookies. Place on ungreased cookie sheets. Bake in a 375°F oven about 7 minutes or until edges are firm and just beginning to brown. Transfer cookies to wire racks and let cool.

**If desired,** spread and/or pipe Royal Icing on cookies. If desired, use Royal Icing to attach pieces of gumdrops. Makes 36 cookies.

**ROYAL ICING:** In a small bowl combine 2 cups powdered sugar, ¼ cup warm water, 4 teaspoons meringue powder, and ¼ teaspoon cream of tartar. Beat with an electric mixer on low speed until combined. Beat on high speed for 7 to 10 minutes or until stiff. Divide in half. To 1 portion, add enough warm water, 1 teaspoon at a time, to make an icing of piping consistency. Color as desired with paste food coloring. Place in pastry bags fitted with decorating tips. To the other portion, add enough warm water, 1 teaspoon at a time, to make an icing of glazing consistency. Color as desired.

**TO STORE:** Place cookies in layers separated by waxed paper in an airtight container; cover. Store cookies at room temperature up to 3 days or freeze unfrosted, undecorated cookies up to 3 months. Thaw the frozen cookies; frost and decorate as desired.

### cookie Q&A

**Q:** Do I need a stand mixer to make these recipes?

**A:** These recipes can be made with portable mixers. When you add the flour, beat in as much as you can using the mixer. Then stir in the remaining flour with a spoon.

**Q:** What kind of cookie sheet should I use?

**A:** Look for shiny, heavy-gauge cookie sheets that have very low or no sides. Avoid dark cookie sheets, which may cause cookie bottoms to overbrown.

**Q:** Can I use a jelly-roll pan to bake cookies?

**A:** Use only if specified—they're generally for bar cookies. Other types of cookies will not brown evenly in a pan with an edge. If you must use a jelly-roll pan, turn it over and bake cookies on bottom of pan.

**Q:** Do I need to let hot cookie sheets cool between batches of cookies?

**A:** Yes. Putting dough on hot cookie sheets may cause cookies to spread and brown too much around the edges. You can avoid this by alternating cookie sheets so they have a chance to cool to room temperature between batches. Also, grease the cookie sheets only if specified in the recipe, and do so only with a light coating of shortening—too much may cause excessive spreading.

106

*Brown Sugar Christmas Cookies*

# Brown Sugar Christmas Cookies

*Jazz up easy drop cookies with irresistible brown sugar and a sprinkling of candies in festive holiday colors.*

- ½ cup butter, softened
- ½ cup shortening
- 1¼ cups packed brown sugar
- ¾ teaspoon baking soda
- ¼ teaspoon salt
- 3 eggs
- 2 teaspoons vanilla
- 3½ cups all-purpose flour
- 1 cup red, green, and white candy-coated milk chocolate bits or red and green candy-coated chocolate pieces
- 1 cup chopped pecans

**In a large mixing bowl** beat butter and shortening with an electric mixer on medium to high speed for 30 seconds. Add brown sugar, baking soda, and salt. Beat until combined, scraping sides of bowl occasionally. Beat in eggs and vanilla until combined. Beat in as much of the flour as you can with the mixer. Stir in any remaining flour, the chocolate bits, and pecans with a wooden spoon.

**Drop dough** by rounded teaspoons 2 inches apart onto an ungreased cookie sheet. If desired, flatten slightly with fingers. Bake in a 375°F oven for 8 to 10 minutes or until edges are lightly browned. Transfer cookies to a wire rack and let cool. Makes about 60 cookies.

**TO STORE:** Place in layers separated by waxed paper in an airtight container; cover. Store at room temperature up to 3 days or freeze up to 3 months.

# Candy Bar Brownies

*Peanut butter and chocolate are an ever-favorite candy-bar combo. Layer the ingredients into a bar cookie, and you'll get a more sophisticated sweet.*

- 1¼ cups finely crushed graham crackers (about 18 crackers)
- ¼ cup sugar
- ¼ cup finely chopped dry-roasted peanuts
- ½ cup butter, melted
- ½ cup butter
- 2 ounces unsweetened chocolate, chopped
- 1 cup sugar
- 2 eggs
- 1 teaspoon vanilla
- ⅔ cup all-purpose flour
- ½ cup chopped peanuts
- 1 recipe Peanut Butter Frosting
- ¼ cup honey-roasted peanuts or regular peanuts

**For crust,** in a medium bowl combine graham crackers, the ¼ cup sugar, and the ¼ cup finely chopped peanuts. Stir in the ½ cup melted butter. Press mixture evenly into the bottom of an ungreased 11×7×1½-inch baking pan. Bake in a 350°F oven for 5 minutes; cool.

*Candy Bar Brownies*

*Chocolate Coconut Tassies*

**For filling,** in a large heavy saucepan melt the ½ cup butter and chocolate over low heat, stirring occasionally. Remove from heat; stir in the 1 cup sugar, eggs, and vanilla just until combined. Stir in flour and the ½ cup chopped peanuts. Spread evenly over crust.

**Bake in the 350°F oven** for 20 minutes more. Cool completely in pan on a wire rack. Spread with Peanut Butter Frosting. Cut into small squares. (Or cut into 24 larger bars.) Place a few honey-roasted peanuts on each square. If desired, place each brownie in a small candy cup. Makes 50 to 70 small brownies.

**PEANUT BUTTER FROSTING:** In a mixing bowl beat ¼ cup softened butter and 2 tablespoons peanut butter with an electric mixer on low speed for 30 seconds. Gradually add 1 cup powdered sugar, beating well. Beat in 1 tablespoon milk and ½ teaspoon vanilla. Gradually beat in 1 cup additional powdered sugar and enough milk to make a frosting of spreading consistency.

**TO STORE:** Cover and store at room temperature up to 3 days. To freeze, wrap unfrosted bars in heavy foil. Freeze up to 3 months. Thaw; frost and cut into bars.

# Chocolate Coconut Tassies

*These two-bite tarts combine rich cream-cheese pastry with luscious coconut-and-pecan filling. They're stunning as gifts but also make lovely no-fork nibbles on a holiday party buffet.*

>     2  ounces sweet baking chocolate, cut up
>     2  3-ounce packages cream cheese, softened
>     ⅓  cup butter, softened
>     1  cup all-purpose flour
>     ⅓  cup sugar
>     2  teaspoons vanilla
>     1  cup flaked coconut
>     ½  cup chopped pecans, toasted
>     2  ounces sweet baking chocolate, cut up (optional)

**In a small saucepan** heat and stir the 2 ounces chocolate over low heat until melted. Cool slightly, 10 to 15 minutes. In a medium bowl beat melted chocolate, 3 ounces of the cream cheese, and butter with an electric mixer on medium speed until combined. Beat in flour until combined. If necessary, cover with plastic wrap and chill in the refrigerator about

1 hour or until dough is easy to handle.

**On a lightly floured surface,** roll dough until ⅛ inch thick. Cut with a 2½-inch scalloped cutter. Place a round in each cup of 1¾-inch muffin pans; press against bottom and sides. (Or omit rolling and divide dough into 30 pieces; shape into balls. Place a ball in each 1¾-inch muffin cup. Press onto bottoms and up sides of muffin cups.) Set aside.

**For filling,** in another bowl beat remaining cream cheese, sugar, and vanilla until smooth. Stir in coconut and pecans. Spoon into crusts in muffin cups, dividing mixture evenly. Bake in a 325°F oven about 20 minutes or until filling begins to brown on top. Cool in muffin cups. Remove from pans and transfer to wire racks; let cool.

**If desired,** in a small saucepan melt the 2 ounces chocolate; cool slightly. Drizzle over tassies. Chill in the refrigerator about 20 minutes or until chocolate is set. Makes 30 tassies.

**TO STORE:** Place in an airtight container in the refrigerator up to 3 days or freeze up to 2 weeks. Thaw before serving.

107

*Elf Hats*

*Lemon Drops*

# Elf Hats

*For a delectable contrast, a crisp, airy meringue gets a rich chocolaty rim and a sprinkling of nuts. Top it off with a dot of tinted icing to add a little whimsy to these elegant treats.*

> 2 egg whites
> ½ teaspoon vanilla
> ⅛ teaspoon cream of tartar
>   Green or red food coloring
>     (optional)
> ⅔ cup sugar
> 6 ounces bittersweet chocolate or
>     semisweet chocolate,
>     chopped
> ¾ cup finely chopped walnuts
>   Purchased decorator icing
>     (optional)

**In a medium mixing bowl** let egg whites stand, covered, at room temperature for 30 minutes. Grease cookie sheets; set aside.

**Add vanilla,** cream of tartar, and if desired, 2 or 3 drops food coloring to egg whites. Beat with an electric mixer on medium speed until soft peaks form (tips curl). Gradually add sugar, 1 tablespoon at a time, beating on high speed about 5 minutes or until stiff, glossy peaks form (tips stand straight).

**Using a decorating bag** fitted with a ½-inch round tip, pipe mixture into small 1-inch-high mounds that end in an angled tip about 1 inch apart on prepared cookie sheets. Place cookie sheets on oven racks in a 300°F oven. Turn off oven and let cookies dry in oven with door closed for 1 hour or until dry and crisp but still light in color. Let cool on cookie sheets. Gently remove cookies.

**In a small heavy saucepan** melt chocolate over low heat, stirring frequently. When cookies are cool, dip bottoms into melted chocolate, then into chopped walnuts. Place on waxed paper; let stand until chocolate is set. If desired, add a dot of colored icing to each tip. Makes about 48 cookies.

**TO STORE:** Place undipped cookies in an airtight container; cover. Store at room temperature up to 3 days or freeze up to 3 months. Just before serving, dip in melted chocolate, then in nuts.

# Lemon Drops

*Sweet, yes—but tart and tingly too! These pretty gems add color, sparkle, and a refreshing zing to your cookie tray.*

> ½ cup butter, softened
> ¾ cup granulated sugar
> 4 teaspoons finely shredded
>     lemon peel
> ½ teaspoon baking powder
> ½ teaspoon baking soda
> ⅛ teaspoon salt
> 1 egg
> ½ cup dairy sour cream
> ⅓ cup lemon juice
> 2 cups all-purpose flour
> 1 recipe Lemon Glaze
>   Coarse sugar
>   Yellow gumdrops, chopped

**In a large mixing bowl** beat butter with an electric mixer on medium to high speed for 30 seconds. Add the granulated sugar, lemon peel, baking powder, baking soda, and salt. Beat until combined, scraping sides of bowl occasionally. Beat in egg, sour cream, and lemon juice until combined. Beat in as much of the flour as you can with

*White Chocolate and Raspberry Cookies*

the mixer. Stir in any remaining flour with a wooden spoon.

**Drop dough** by slightly rounded tablespoons 3 inches apart onto an ungreased cookie sheet. Bake in a 375°F oven about 8 minutes or until tops are firm. Transfer cookies to a wire rack. Brush the tops of the warm cookies with Lemon Glaze. Sprinkle with coarse sugar and decorate with chopped gumdrops. Let cookies cool. Makes about 36 cookies.

**LEMON GLAZE:** In a small bowl stir together ¼ cup granulated sugar and 2 tablespoons lemon juice.

**TO STORE:** Place in layers separated by waxed paper in an airtight container; cover. Store at room temperature up to 3 days or freeze up to 3 months.

# White Chocolate and Raspberry Cookies

*Raspberries and white chocolate find their way into many a spectacular dessert, so why not a cookie like these?*

|     |                                              |
| --- | -------------------------------------------- |
| 8   | ounces white baking bars or white chocolate baking squares |
| ½   | cup butter, softened                         |
| 1   | cup sugar                                    |
| 1   | teaspoon baking soda                         |
| ¼   | teaspoon salt                                |
| 2   | eggs                                         |
| 2¾  | cups all-purpose flour                       |
| ½   | cup seedless raspberry jam                   |
| 3   | ounces white baking bars or white chocolate baking squares |
| ½   | teaspoon shortening                          |

**Grease** a large cookie sheet; set aside. Chop 4 ounces of the white baking bars; set aside. In a small heavy saucepan melt remaining 4 ounces baking bars over low heat, stirring constantly; cool.

**In a large mixing bowl** beat butter with an electric mixer on medium to high speed for 30 seconds. Add sugar, baking soda, and salt. Beat until combined, scraping sides of bowl occasionally. Beat

in eggs and melted baking bars until combined. Beat in as much of the flour as you can with the mixer. Stir in any remaining flour with a wooden spoon. Stir in the 4 ounces chopped baking bars (dough will be stiff).

**Drop dough** by rounded teaspoons 2 inches apart onto the prepared cookie sheet. Bake in a 375°F oven for 7 to 9 minutes or until edges are lightly browned. Cool on cookie sheet for 1 minute. Transfer cookies to a wire rack and let cool.

**Before serving,** in a small heavy saucepan melt jam over low heat. Spoon about ½ teaspoon jam over each cookie. In another small heavy saucepan melt the remaining 3 ounces white baking bars and shortening over low heat, stirring constantly. Drizzle over cookies; let stand until set. (If necessary, chill cookies for 15 minutes or until drizzle is set.) Makes about 48 cookies.

**TO STORE:** Place cookies in layers separated by waxed paper in an airtight container; cover. Store in refrigerator up to 3 days or freeze plain cookies up to 3 months. Thaw cookies; top with jam. Drizzle with melted baking bars mixture.

109

*cookie* Q&A

Q: Can I substitute margarine for butter in cookies?

A: Butter's best—nothing comes close to the flavor and richness it brings to cookies; it also contributes to their texture and browning. However, if you wish to substitute margarine, buy only stick margarine with at least 80 percent vegetable oil. If the oil content does not appear on the front of the package, check the nutrition label; the margarine you use should have at least 100 calories per each tablespoon.

Bourbon Balls

# boxes of beauty

**The sharing of sweets** is a beloved holiday tradition. This year make it last a little longer than usual. Tuck the handmade gems inside exquisite handcrafted boxes the recipient will use and cherish after the goodies inside have disappeared.

## Bourbon Balls

*Just a tipple of bourbon deepens the flavor of these nutty, chocolaty, (and super-easy) candies.*

  1  cup semisweet chocolate pieces
 ¼  cup sugar
  3  tablespoons light-colored corn syrup
 ⅓  cup bourbon
2½  cups finely crushed vanilla wafers (about 55 wafers)
 ½  cup finely chopped walnuts
     Unsweetened cocoa powder, coarse sugar, and/or powdered sugar

**In a medium heavy saucepan** cook and stir chocolate over low heat until chocolate is melted. Remove from heat. **Stir in sugar and corn syrup.** Add bourbon; stir until mixed. Add vanilla wafers and walnuts to chocolate mixture; stir until mixed. Let stand about 30 minutes.

**Shape mixture** into 1-inch balls. Roll in cocoa powder, coarse sugar, and/or powdered sugar to coat. Store in a tightly covered container up to 1 week. Makes about 50 balls.

## Milk Chocolate and Caramel Clusters

*This candy will harden if allowed to sit too long, so it's best to eat it the day it's made. That's a great reason to pop by a friend's house and enjoy the gift together. Hint: Work quickly when dropping the candies onto the cookie sheets so the mixture doesn't harden in the saucepan.*

12  vanilla caramels
 ½  cup milk chocolate pieces
  2  tablespoons water
  2  cups honey graham cereal, slightly crushed (about 1½ cups)
 ¾  cup peanuts

**Line cookie sheets** with waxed paper; set aside.

**In a medium heavy saucepan** combine the caramels, milk chocolate pieces, and water. Stir over low heat until caramels are melted. Remove from heat. Stir in cereal and peanuts.

**Working quickly,** drop mixture from a teaspoon onto prepared cookie sheets. Let stand until firm (about 30 minutes). Makes about 28 clusters.

## extra touches

Papier-mâché and wooden boxes become elegant gift containers when decked out in pretty papers and flowers.

### BOUQUET BOX

Cut a strip of decorative paper to fit the side of the box and glue it in place with spray adhesive, piecing it as needed. To line the lid and box, trace the pieces onto paper and cut out two circles adding ¼ inch all around. Slash in ¼ inch around the circles. Glue the circles in place, letting the slashed portions go up the side of the box or lid. Cut bands to fit the inside edges and glue them in place. Using hot glue, attach ribbon to the rim of the lid. Glue paper roses, leaves, and jingle bells to the lid top, covering it completely.

NOTE: Make sure all materials that will be in contact with food are nontoxic.

## *extra touches*

### RIBBON AND FLOWERS BOX

■ Remove all the hardware from a hinged wooden box and paint it as desired. Glue ribbon down the center of the top and bottom, wrapping it to the inside. Line the box bottom and lid with paper as described for the Bouquet Box on *page 111*. Reassemble the box. Make two sprays of berries and glue one to each side of the lid's ribbon. Fold additional ribbon into graduated loops and staple it at the center to hold it in place. Trim the ends. Glue the bow over the berry sprays. Add small pinecones, rosebuds, and silver branches to the spray. NOTE: Make sure all materials that will be in contact with any food are nontoxic.

*Easy Layered Fudge
and
Easy White Chocolate Candies*

## Easy Layered Fudge

*Fudge is always luscious, but it's not always the prettiest candy in the box. Here white baking bar striped atop the chocolate base gives the candy a striking layered look.*

18 ounces bittersweet chocolate, chopped
2 14-ounce cans sweetened condensed milk
1 cup chopped almonds, toasted
1 teaspoon vanilla
3 cups white baking pieces
2 tablespoons orange liqueur (optional)
2 teaspoons finely shredded orange peel
Finely chopped almonds (optional)

**Line** a 13×9×2-inch baking pan with foil, extending the foil over the edges of the pan. Butter foil; set aside.

**In a medium heavy saucepan** cook and stir chocolate and 1 can sweetened condensed milk over low heat just until chocolate melts and mixture is smooth. Remove saucepan from heat. Stir in the 1 cup almonds and vanilla.

**Spread** and press chocolate mixture evenly in the prepared pan. Cover and chill while preparing white layer.

**In another medium saucepan** cook and stir the white baking pieces and 1 can sweetened condensed milk over low heat just until pieces melt and mixture is smooth. Remove saucepan from heat. Stir in orange liqueur, if using, and the orange peel.

**Spread** white mixture evenly over chocolate mixture in pan. If desired, sprinkle with finely chopped almonds, pressing lightly into white layer. Cover and chill for 2 hours or until firm.

**When fudge is firm,** use foil to lift it out of pan. Cut fudge into about 1-inch pieces. Store tightly covered at room temperature or in the refrigerator up to 1 week. Makes about 4 pounds (about 96 pieces).

## Easy White Chocolate Candies

*Here's a candy even the truest amateurs can prepare! Just melt white baking pieces into foil-lined cups, and sprinkle with an assortment of colorful toppings. That's all there is to it—and the results are exquisite.*

1 12-ounce package white baking pieces
30 foil or sturdy paper miniature candy cups
¾ cup assorted coarsely chopped dried fruits, such as dried apricots, dried cranberries, and golden raisins, and/or nuts, such as walnuts, pecans, almonds, and pistachio nuts

**In a small saucepan** cook and stir baking pieces over low heat until melted. Remove from heat. Spoon melted baking pieces into candy cups (about 1 rounded teaspoon per cup). Immediately sprinkle tops with dried fruits and/or nuts; press lightly into melted baking pieces.

**Chill in the refrigerator** about 30 minutes or until firm. Store in a covered container at room temperature up to 1 week. Makes 30 candies.

112

# Hazelnut-Chocolate Truffles

*Looking for an all-out dazzler? Something about hazelnuts and chocolate always spells opulence. The duo is rolled into a liqueur-infused truffle and tucked into a stunning handcrafted candy box. One luxurious gift indeed.*

| | |
|---|---|
| 16 | ounces white baking pieces (2⅔ cups) |
| ⅓ | cup whipping cream |
| 1 | cup chopped hazelnuts (filberts), toasted |
| 2 | tablespoons white crème de cacao (optional) |
| 18 | ounces semisweet chocolate pieces (3 cups) |
| 3 | tablespoons shortening |
| 2 | cups finely chopped hazelnuts (filberts), toasted |

**For filling,** in a medium saucepan cook and stir white baking pieces and whipping cream over low heat just until baking pieces are melted. Remove from heat. Stir in the 1 cup chopped hazelnuts and crème de cacao, if using. Cover; place in freezer for 1½ to 2 hours or until firm. Divide filling into 48 portions (about a rounded measuring teaspoon); shape each portion into about a 1-inch ball. Freeze 15 minutes.

**Meanwhile,** in a 4-cup glass measure combine semisweet chocolate pieces and shortening. In a large glass bowl pour very warm tap water (110°F to 120°F) to a depth of 1 inch. Place glass measure with semisweet chocolate inside large bowl. (Water should cover bottom half of the glass measure.) Stir semisweet chocolate constantly with a rubber spatula until chocolate is completely melted and smooth. This takes about 15 to 20 minutes; don't rush. If water cools, remove glass measure. Discard cool water; add warm water. Return glass measure to bowl with water. **Using a fork,** dip frozen balls, 1 at a time, into melted chocolate. Tap fork

## extra touches

### ROSE-TOP BOX

■ Cut a strip of decorative paper to fit the side of the box and glue it in place with spray adhesive, piecing it as needed. To line the box, trace the box onto paper and cut the shape adding ¼ inch all around. Slash in ¼ inch around the edge. Glue the piece to the bottom, letting the slashed portions go up the side of the box. Cut a band to fit the inside edge and glue it in place. Cover both the inside and outside of the lid in the same manner. Using hot glue, attach braid to the rim of the lid, turning under the raw edges. Glue a single large rose, silk leaves, and small gold ornaments to the top, positioning the arrangement to one side of the lid.

NOTE: Make sure all materials that will be in contact with food are nontoxic.

against the rim of the measure to remove excess chocolate. Roll in the finely chopped hazelnuts.* Place on a baking sheet lined with waxed paper. Freeze for 15 minutes. Store, tightly covered, up to 3 days at room temperature or 1 week in the refrigerator. Makes 48 truffles.

*\*NOTE:* If desired, instead of rolling chocolate-dipped truffles in hazelnuts, place the dipped truffles on a baking sheet lined with waxed paper. Sprinkle tops with finely chopped toasted hazelnuts (you will need about 1 cup total). Freeze as above.

113

◀ Citrus Cups: When a heavy dessert just won't do after a holiday meal, these dashing citrus cups end dinner on a lighter note. Simply use a sharp knife to hollow out citrus fruits (limes, lemons, small oranges) and add a scoop of ice cream or sherbet. Serve in glasses or cups. If desired, support the curved base of the fruit with coarse sugar and garnish with citrus peel strips and mint.

# In a Twinkling:
# citrus for the season

◀ Spice Mix for Mulled Wine or Cider: This gift makes a delicious mulled beverage. To make: Use a vegetable peeler to remove long strips of peel from 2 oranges. Scrape off any white portion. Arrange a single layer of strips on a baking sheet lined with parchment paper. Bake in a 200°F oven about 10 minutes or until peel is dry but still pliable. For each spice mix, combine 2 or 3 orange peel strips, ¼ cup dried cranberries, 2 cinnamon sticks, and 2 tablespoons crystallized ginger in a small food-safe container. Cover with food-safe wrap. If desired, trim with decorative items. Store at room temperature up to 1 month. (For 8 spice mixes, use 2 oranges, 2 cups dried cranberries, 16 cinnamon sticks, and 1 cup crystallized ginger.) For tag and instructions to give with gift, see page 156.

Kumquats are among the most miniature of citrus fruits, and when frozen solid, they can stand in for ice cubes. Not only are they more festive and colorful than the usual clear cube, they also won't water down your drink as they thaw.

◄ Citrus butter adds a seasonal accent to the breads you serve at the holidays. To make: In a small mixing bowl beat ½ cup softened butter or margarine, 1 tablespoon powdered sugar, 1 teaspoon finely shredded lemon peel or orange peel, and 2 teaspoons lemon juice or 1 tablespoon orange juice with an electric mixer on medium to high speed until light and fluffy. Cover and chill at least 1 hour to blend flavors. To serve, let stand at room temperature about 30 minutes or until soft enough to spread.

115

◄ Citrus syrup makes a zippy-sweet gift for pancake- and waffle-loving friends. It also easily transforms into a thinner syrup used to mix a festive, nonalcoholic sipper you can serve throughout the season. To make: In a medium saucepan combine 2 teaspoons finely shredded orange peel, 1 cup orange juice, 2 tablespoons lemon juice, and ½ cup sugar. Bring to boiling over medium-high heat, stirring occasionally. Reduce heat and simmer, uncovered, about 15 minutes or until reduced to ¾ cup to use in a spritzer or about 20 minutes or until reduced to ½ cup to use as a waffle syrup, stirring mixture occasionally. Serve warm or cool. Cover and refrigerate remaining syrup up to 1 week.

# a spanish brunch

*Cava Granada Cocktail
and
Cured Olives and
Manchego Cheese*

# on new year's day

This year, fête your friends with a Spanish-inspired brunch that touches on so many of Spain's well-loved ingredients and specialties: grapes, olives, Manchego cheese, Serrano ham, and the famous Spanish potato omelet. Toast it all with a glass of cava. *Salud!*

Looking for a new way to ring in the New Year? Take inspiration from Spain. In the past few years, Spanish cuisine has been turning heads among food lovers everywhere. And no wonder! While the vast majority of Spanish cooking is straightforward, home-style fare, it's anything but ordinary, blending simple preparations with fresh foods for a cooking style that's dynamic, diverse, and unforgettably good.

First, a word about ingredients: One thing that makes Spanish cooking so notable is not fancy, difficult techniques, but top-shelf ingredients. This is the occasion to get out your high-quality olive oil, replace the two-year-old tin of paprika with a fresh one, and head to the gourmet shop for true Manchego cheese and imported Serrano ham (or substitute the more widely available Italian prosciutto). This menu's fantastic ingredients are the key to a meal your guests will long remember.

## Cured Olives and Manchego Cheese

*Spain's most popular cheese, Manchego, is a mild-flavored sheep's milk cheese with a firm, dry texture—well suited to a robe of fruity olive oil. Manchego is widely available in U.S. markets.*

- 1 small fennel bulb
- 4 ounces Manchego cheese, cut into 1-inch pieces
- 2 cloves garlic
- 2 teaspoons fennel seeds
- ¼ teaspoon crushed red pepper
- 1 cup pitted green olives
- ½ cup olive oil
- 1 tablespoon lemon juice
  Baguette-style French bread, sliced and lightly toasted, if desired

**Remove stalks,** wilted outer layers, base, and core from fennel bulb. Cut fennel into 1-inch pieces; set aside. In a food processor* place cheese (cheese should be cold from the refrigerator). Cover and process with several on/off turns until finely chopped. Place chopped cheese in a medium bowl. Add fennel bulb to food processor. Cover and process with several on/off turns until finely chopped. Add to bowl with cheese; set aside.

**With food processor running,** drop garlic, fennel seeds, and crushed red pepper through feed tube; process until garlic is finely minced. Add olives; process until finely chopped.

**Add olive mixture,** oil, and lemon juice to cheese mixture; stir well. Cover and chill in the refrigerator overnight. Let stand at room temperature for 1 hour before serving. To serve, spoon some of the mixture onto bread slices. Cover and chill any remaining cheese-olive mixture up to 2 days. Makes about 2 cups.

**\*Note:** If you do not have a food processor, use a knife to finely chop the ingredients.

## Cava Granada Cocktail

*The Spanish named their sparkling wine "cava" and their word for pomegranate is "granada." The city Granada was named for the fruit, which arrived in Spain around 800 A.D. Mix the two for a festive holiday drink.*

- 1 tablespoon pomegranate seeds
- ¾ cup cava or other sparkling wine, chilled

**For each cocktail,** place the pomegranate seeds in a stemmed wine flute. Pour cava over fruit and serve. Makes 1 (6-ounce) serving.

*Spanish Omelet (Tortilla) with Potato, Spanish Onion, and Serrano Ham and Orange, Red Grape, and Watercress Salad*

# Spanish Omelet (Tortilla) with Potato, Spanish Onion, and Serrano Ham

*Tortillas are a uniquely Spanish spin on omelet making. Once mastered, the technique can be used with a variety of ingredients for a simple brunch or light dinner entrée. Spanish salt-cured ham (Jamon Serrano) recently appeared in U.S. markets. If you can't find Serrano ham, Italian prosciutto is an excellent substitute.*

    1  pound potatoes, peeled and
         cut into ½-inch cubes
    1  cup thinly sliced Spanish onion
         or sweet yellow onion
    ¼  teaspoon salt
    ¼  cup olive oil
    6  eggs
    ½  teaspoon ground black pepper
    ¼  teaspoon salt
    4  ounces thinly sliced Serrano
         ham or prosciutto, cut into
         bite-size strips
       Chopped tomatoes
       Fresh chives

**In a large nonstick skillet** with flared sides cook potatoes, onion, and the ¼ teaspoon salt in hot oil over medium heat for 20 to 25 minutes or until tender and starting to brown; stir occasionally. Drain vegetables in colander set over a bowl, reserving drained oil. Cool vegetables slightly, about 15 minutes.

**Meanwhile,** in a large mixing bowl lightly whisk together eggs, pepper, and the ¼ teaspoon salt; stir in ham and cooled potato mixture.

**In the same skillet** heat 1 tablespoon reserved oil over medium-low heat; discard remaining oil. Pour egg mixture into skillet. Cook about 15 minutes until sides are set; center may appear slightly moist. Run a spatula underneath mixture occasionally to prevent sticking.

**Carefully slide** omelet onto a large heatproof plate. Invert skillet over omelet; holding skillet and plate together, flip omelet back into skillet. Use a spatula to tuck under any uneven edges. Cook for 10 minutes more. Slide omelet onto a clean serving plate. Let stand for 10 minutes before slicing into wedges. Serve within 1 hour. Garnish with tomatoes and chives. Makes 4 servings.

# Almond-Hazelnut Cookies

*Cookies made with finely ground nuts and little, if any, flour are popular throughout Spain.*

¾ cup sugar
1 cup finely ground almonds*
½ cup finely ground skinless** toasted hazelnuts (filberts)*
½ teaspoon finely shredded orange peel
¼ teaspoon ground nutmeg
2 egg whites
2 egg yolks
¼ cup sliced almonds
2 tablespoons finely chopped skinless* toasted hazelnuts (filberts)

**Line 2 cookie sheets** with parchment paper or nonstick foil; set aside. In a large mixing bowl combine sugar, ground almonds, ground hazelnuts, orange peel, and nutmeg; set aside.

**In a medium mixing bowl** beat egg whites with an electric mixer on high speed until stiff peaks form. Beat in egg yolks using low speed. Fold egg mixture into sugar-nut mixture.

**Drop by rounded teaspoons** 3 inches apart on prepared cookie sheets; sprinkle cookies with sliced almonds and chopped hazelnuts.

**Bake in a 350°F oven** for 10 to 12 minutes or until lightly browned. Cool completely on cookie sheets. Peel cookies off paper and store in an airtight container. If desired, serve with chocolate ice cream. Makes about 24 cookies.

*NOTE: Start with 1½ cups almonds to get the 1 cup ground almonds; ¾ cup hazelnuts to get the ½ cup ground hazelnuts; and about 3 tablespoons hazelnuts to get the 2 tablespoons finely chopped hazelnuts. To grind the nuts, place nuts in a food processor or blender. Cover and process or blend until nuts are just ground.

*Almond-Hazelnut Cookies*

**NOTE: To toast and remove skins from hazelnuts, place nuts in a shallow baking pan. Bake, uncovered, in a 350°F oven for 8 to 10 minutes or until lightly toasted, stirring twice. Turn hot nuts out onto a clean kitchen towel; cool slightly. Cover nuts with the towel and gently roll in towel to remove skins. Cool completely.

# Orange, Red Grape, and Watercress Salad

*To make it an authentic treat, pick up Spanish olive oil, sherry vinegar, and sweet roasted paprika at a specialty food shop. Or, for an everyday salad, use everyday pantry ingredients.*

3 tablespoons olive oil
1 tablespoon Spanish sherry vinegar or red wine vinegar
¼ teaspoon sea salt
⅛ teaspoon paprika

3 seedless oranges, peeled and sliced
1 cup seedless red grapes, halved
4 cups watercress, arugula, or fresh spinach
¼ cup fresh mint leaves*
Paprika
Cracked black pepper

**For dressing,** in medium bowl whisk together first 4 ingredients. Carefully stir in fruit. Cover; chill at least 1 hour.

**Discard stems** from watercress; place greens in salad bowl. Tear large mint leaves into smaller pieces; leave small mint leaves whole. Add mint to salad bowl.

**To serve,** drain dressing from fruit; pour dressing over greens. Toss lightly to coat. Divide among 8 salad plates; arrange fruit on top. Sprinkle with paprika and pepper. Makes 8 servings.

*NOTE: If fresh mint is not available, stir ½ teaspoon dried mint, crushed, into the oil-vinegar dressing.

Little luxuries are what we often

**skip for ourselves** Pamper your friends and family with these fun extras that make them feel oh-so-special. From personal items like high-style handbags to romantic candles and pretty accents for their homes, when it comes to gift giving, it's often the little things in life that count.

# GIVING

## *from the* HEART

give a hand

# From evening bags to everyday workhorses, handcrafted handbags are hot this season.

## to-go boxes

These bags are smokin'! Decorated wooden boxes—often called cigar box bags—are the rage in high-style boutiques. Personalize the purchased boxes to give each a distinct personality.

### FOR ALL BOXES:
Remove any existing hardware and sand all the box surfaces. Wipe with a tack cloth. Apply primer, sand, and wipe again.

### FOR THE DECOUPAGE FRENCH TOURIST BOX:
1 Cut the main paper large enough to fit the top and sides of each box piece and wrap to the inside. To finish the inside of the box, cut paper to fit the inside top and bottom and go partway up the sides. Cut bands to fit the sides of the box.

2 Starting with the front piece, apply decoupage medium to the wrong side of the paper. Wrap the paper around the box as if wrapping a package. Miter and splice the corners as needed and trim any excess paper. Wrap the paper's margins to the inside. Apply decoupage medium as needed. Repeat for the back piece.

3 Fit the inside front and back papers to the corresponding box pieces. Clip into the corners so the paper fits flatly against the main portion of the box and goes up the sides. Trim away any excess at the corners and decoupage the papers in place.

4 Decoupage the side bands to the inside front and back pieces, covering the margins left from the previous papers. The entire box should now be covered in paper. Apply four or more coats of decoupage medium to all surfaces. Sand very lightly between coats, letting each coat dry before applying the next one.

5 Arrange stickers, rub-on transfers, letters, and other flat trims as desired to the box front. Add two more coats of decoupage medium.

6 Reassemble the box and add any additional hardware needed. Thread the beads onto the handle. Place an Eiffel Tower charm in the middle of the handle. See the photograph *below left* for details. Attach the handle to the box.

7 Glue the three-dimensional trims, braid, and corner pieces in place. See the photograph *opposite* for detail. If desired, glue a small mirror to the inside of the front. Glue trim around the edges of the mirror.

### FOR THE PAINTED QUOTATIONS BOX:
1 Paint the box at least two coats of white paint, sanding lightly between coats. Cut phrases from the vellum sheets.

2 Arrange the phrases on the box. Apply decoupage medium to the back of the phrase pieces and smooth them onto the box. Apply at least four coats of decoupage medium to the outside surfaces. NOTE: The vellum may wrinkle when the decoupage medium is applied but it should smooth out as it dries.

3 Reassemble the box and add any additional hardware needed. Thread the beads onto the handle and attach the handle to the box lid. If desired, glue a mirror to the inside of the lid. Glue trim around the edges of the mirror.

4 Trim a final saying to fit the vellum tag and decoupage it to the tag front. Place a brad through the opening of the tag and fold back the ends. Glue the tag to the box.

123

# for the birds

❧ This fun bag tickles almost anyone's fashion fancy. Feather trim spirals around a faux-suede bag and is capped with ruffled ribbon.

**1** With wrong sides facing, sew the fabric pieces together along the sides and bottom to form the purse. Leave one short end open.

**2** Pinch one corner of the purse together, matching the side and bottom seams. Sew across this point at a 45-degree angle. Repeat for the other side. This will create a flat 1½-inch-wide bottom for the bag.

**3** Fold down the top of the bag 2 inches. Working from the inside of the bag, fuse the top hem in place with iron-on fabric tape. Turn the bag right side out.

**4** Cut two 20-inch lengths of ribbon for handle covers. To prevent fraying, cut the ribbon with a woodburning tool or run a thin bead of fabric glue along the cut edge. With right sides facing, sew along the long edge of each ribbon. Turn to the right side.

**5** Remove one end from each handle piece and shirr a ribbon tube over the handle. Replace the end piece. Position a handle on one side of the bag. Sew buttons over the handle ends to secure. See the photo *above* for details. Repeat for the other side, aligning the handles with those on the first side.

**6** Starting at the front left seam of the bag and ending at the right side seam, spiral the feather trim around the bag. Glue it in place.

**7** Using a gathering stitch, sew down the center of the remaining ribbon. Draw up the gathers to create a ruffle the same length as the feather trim. Glue the ribbon over the top band of the feather trim.

# ornamental tote

❧ Brighten up your holiday shopping with a purchased canvas bag that's trimmed with ornaments cut from felt. Make smaller versions for gift bags.

**1** Enlarge the patterns on *page 156* to scale. Cut five ornaments from felt. Arrange the ornaments on the bag. Using the fabric marker, trace around the top of each ornament to mark its position. Set the ornaments aside.

**2** Cut lengths of ribbon to reach from under the ornaments to the top of the bag and 2 inches inside the bag. Glue the ribbons in place.

**3** Glue the ornaments in place. Using glitter pens, fill in the ornament cap sections. Add lines and dots for further embellishment. Let the glitter dry completely.

# organdy flower pin

∾ Single-flower "corsages" are making a comeback as fashion-forward lapel pins. Those made from organdy ribbon have a soft, feminine feel.

**1** Using a 24-inch length of organdy ribbon, sew a gathering stitch along entire length of ribbon. Pull the thread to gather.

**2** To create the flower center, tightly roll one end of the organdy ribbon onto itself. Stitch into place. Spiral the ribbon around the stitched edge at center, forming a flower shape. Stitch into place as you go.

**3** When the flower is at the desired fullness, clip off the excess ribbon and sew the end in place.

Enlarge the leaf pattern on *page 157* to scale. Cut four silk leaves. Sew them together in pairs with right sides facing, leaving the bottom open. Turn and press.

# flower power

Impress your friends with your own version of the high-style posy pins popping up in stores and catalogs.

Using a ¼-inch seam allowance, sew the pairs of fabric circles together around the outer edge with right sides facing. Fold the circles in half and cut along the fold line. Discard one of the half-circles and work with the remainder.

Sew the remaining petals around the center petal shingle-style so the flat edge of each new petal meets the end of the previous petal. See the photograph *above* for details. If desired, add a length of gathered organdy ribbon.

[6] Enlarge the leaf pattern on *page 197* to scale. Cut four leaves. Sew them together in pairs with right sides facing, leaving the bottom open. Turn and press.

[7] Lay one leaf shape on the other with a ⅜-inch overlap. Sew the leaves together along the open ends. See the photograph *opposite* for details. Form pleats as shown *far left*. Sew the leaves to the flower.

Lay one leaf shape on the other with a ⅜-inch overlap. Sew the leaves together along the open ends. See the photograph *opposite* for details. Form pleats as shown *above*. Sew the leaves to the flower.

[6] To create a stamen, wrap one end of a 1½-inch length of wire through a seed bead. Slide a large bead and then seed beads onto the wire. Make a loop at the end of the wire. Repeat to make three stamens. Working from the back of the flower, sew the stamens to the flower center. Sew a pin back onto the back of the flower.

Clip into the seam allowance on the five half circles. Turn half circles inside out and press. Sew two rows of basting stitch along open edge. Pull top two threads to evenly gather the circles into petals. See the photograph *above* for details.

[8] To create a stamen, wrap one end of a 1½-inch length of wire through a seed bead. Slide a large bead and then seed beads onto the wire. Make a loop at the end of the wire. Repeat to make three stamens. Working from the back of the flower, sew the stamens to the flower center. Sew a pin back onto the back of the flower.

# fabric flower pin

❧ For a less romantic look that suits the work world, use taffeta instead of organdy for the pin's flower petals.

[1] Fold the fabric in half, with right sides facing. Using a 6-inch bowl, trace three circles onto the fabric. With pinking shears, cut six 6-inch circles of fabric. See the photograph *top center* for details.

Form one petal into the flower center by rolling it tightly together. Stitch it in place.

# can-do candles

Lighten up dark winter days for friends and family with handmade and embellished candles that spread a warm glow.

# magic windows

Take a peek at these clever candles. Windows carved from handmade or purchased square pillar candles hide treasures and trinkets inside.

1 Cut off the top of the carton. Cut a notch large enough to accommodate the skewer in the rim of the carton, centering the notch. Cut a matching notch directly across from the first one.

2 Place the wick in the center of the carton and press its metal base into the bottom of the carton. Lay the skewer in the notches. Wrap the end of the wick around the skewer so it remains centered.

3 Pinch one side of the can to form a spout for pouring. Place chunks of wax in the can and sit the can in the saucepan. Add water to the saucepan, making sure the can does not tip or float.

4 Place the saucepan over low heat, letting the warm water melt the wax. Do not leave the wax unattended, stir it, let the can float or tip, or let the water boil. As the wax melts, carefully add more wax. Melt enough wax to fill the carton to one-third the final depth. Add tint to create the desired color.

## What You'll Need...

- [ ] Clean, empty ½-gallon wax-coated cardboard milk carton
- [ ] Waxed candlewick with metal base
- [ ] Skewer or pencil
- [ ] Large clean, empty can
- [ ] Candle wax
- [ ] Sturdy saucepan
- [ ] Candle tint
- [ ] Potholder
- [ ] Card stock or lightweight cardboard scrap
- [ ] Flexible putty knife
- [ ] Heavy gloves
- [ ] Decorative elements such as beads, shaped sequins, and decorative pins
- [ ] Short sequin pins

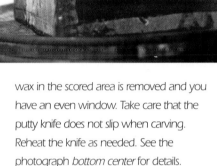

6 Repeat the melting and pouring process two more times, tinting the wax a slightly different color if desired. A divot may form in the center of the candle as it hardens.

7 Let the candle cool and harden completely. This may take a day or more. If a divot forms at this point, fill it with any remaining wax so the top is fairly flat. Carefully peel away the milk carton.

8 Cut a piece of card stock the desired size of the window. Center it on one side of the candle. Using the corner edge of the putty knife, score around the template. Remove the template.

9 Heat the edge of the putty knife over a lit candle. Wearing protective gloves in case the knife slips, gently carve out the scored area until it is an even ¼ inch deep. Work from the edges to the center until all the

wax in the scored area is removed and you have an even window. Take care that the putty knife does not slip when carving. Reheat the knife as needed. See the photograph *bottom center* for details.

10 Arrange beads, shaped sequins, or other decorations in the window. Small items such as seed beads can be allowed to float in the window. Use sequin pins to hold larger items in place. For interest, vary the height of the elements.

Melt a small amount of uncolored wax as described in Step 4. Carefully pour it into the window so it is perfectly even with the sides of the candle. See the photograph *above* for details. Let the wax cool and harden completely. If desired, repeat the process to make windows on other sides of the candle.

Slowly pour the melted wax into the carton. Let the wax harden completely. See the photograph *above* for details

# jazzy fusion

〜 Embossing materials dress an ordinary pillar candle in sheer elegance. An embossing gun fuses stamped tissue to the candle surface for a permanent design. Gold wire and beads add the finishing touch.

1 Cut the dark paper to fit the candle. Dust the paper with the antistatic bag, then stamp it. Brush embossing pigment over the stamping; use a second brush to remove excess pigment.

2 Pin down the paper with tweezers and emboss it with the heat gun. Place the paper over the candle. Working in small sections, use the tweezers and embossing gun to melt the paper into the candle surface.

3 Repeat the embossing process on the light paper. Cut out the designs and fuse them to the first layer of paper. Use the tweezers to hold the small papers in place while using the heat gun.

4 Wrap the candle with wire, twisting the ends to secure it. Curl the tails. Thread the beads onto the head pin and loop the pin end. Attach the bead strand to the twist of the wire with a jump ring.

## What You'll Need...

- [ ] Large-diameter purple pillar candle
- [ ] Dark and light pink tissue paper
- [ ] Embossing antistatic bag
- [ ] Embossing ink pad
- [ ] Small rubber stamps
- [ ] Gold embossing pigment
- [ ] 2 small paintbrushes
- [ ] Long tweezers
- [ ] Embossing heat gun
- [ ] 20-gauge gold wire
- [ ] Head pin and jump ring
- [ ] 2 small gold beads
- [ ] Purple oval glass bead
- [ ] Wire side cutters
- [ ] Round jewelry pliers

# spell it out

What You'll Need...

- [ ] Purchased jar candle
- [ ] Decorative paper
- [ ] Paper crimper
- [ ] Paper ribbon
- [ ] Double-sided tape
- [ ] Three-dimensional scrapbooking letters

State your scent-iments with a message on a bottle—a bottle that holds a purchased candle. Cut decorative paper longer than the circumference of a jar candle and run it through a paper crimper. Cut paper ribbon to fit over the crimped paper. Tape the ribbon to the crimped paper. Tape the crimped paper to the jar candle. Tape letters to the paper ribbon, varying their design and staggering their placement for interest. If the candle has a lid, use scraps to decorate the lid, layering them as desired.

# bits and pieces

Little things often add up to great results. Shards of tile, broken china, or a skein of yarn can yield great gifts.

## marvelous mosaics

～ Get a handle on these designs. Here a broken mug finds a new life on the lid of a trinket box. To collect a mix of mosaic pieces, look for broken tiles at crafts shops and tile stores.

1 Sand the box and wipe it clean. Paint the sides and inside as desired. For a color wash, dilute the paint with water, paint the box, then wipe away the paint so the grain shows through.

2 To break up the tile or china, lay it on one half of an old towel and cover it with the other half. Hit the towel with a hammer to break the tile. Repeat until you have the desired size pieces. NOTE: If you are using china, use only perfectly flat sections. See the photograph *left* for details.

3 Wrap the mug in the towel and carefully hit it close to the handle. It may take several tries to successfully break a handle away from the mug without breaking the handle.

4 Draw the outline of the box onto paper. Starting with tile pieces that have flat outer edges and corners, fit the shards along the box outline. Put the handle in place. Fit the remaining broken pieces and other mosaic elements within the outline, leaving ⅛- to ¼-inch gaps between the shards. Use the hammer or tile nippers to further shape the pieces so they fit. Remove any curved pieces from the base of the handle with tile nippers.

5 Apply tile adhesive to the box top following the manufacturer's directions. Transfer the pieces from the outline to the box top, making adjustments as needed. See the photograph *right* for details. Use industrial-strength glue to hold the handle in place. Let all the pieces dry according to the adhesive manufacturer's instructions.

6 Mix the grout according to the manufacturer's directions. Wearing disposable gloves and using care around the sharp edges, press the grout between the mosaic pieces. Work it into the spaces so the surface is flat and completely covered. See the photograph *above* for details. Let the grout dry according to the manufacturer's directions.

7 Using a damp sponge, wipe away the excess grout. NOTE: Failure to do this will leave a permanent haze over the mosaic. See the photograph *right* for details. If desired, seal the tile with grout sealer.

132

## What You'll Need...

- [ ] Purchased wooden box
- [ ] Fine sandpaper and tack cloth
- [ ] Acrylic paint
- [ ] Paintbrush
- [ ] Clean, lint-free rags
- [ ] Tile, china with flat rims, flat-sided marbles, and other items for mosaic
- [ ] Old towel
- [ ] Hammer
- [ ] Mug or teacup
- [ ] Paper and pencil
- [ ] Tile nippers
- [ ] Tile adhesive
- [ ] Industrial-strength glue
- [ ] Grout and disposable container for mixing
- [ ] Disposable gloves
- [ ] Sponge
- [ ] Grout sealer (optional)

134

## using tassels

Sure, they look great, but what do you do with decorative tassels? Some are functional while others are meant simply to draw the eye to furniture or architectural elements.

SMALL TASSELS

- Hang from ceiling fan pulls
- Slip over the knobs of small wall-hung drawers
- Tie to the end of a chair-pull lamp, switches, or the top finial of a lamp
- Attach thimble-size ones to clothing zippers, handbags, cell phone cases, tote bags, and other items using lanyard clips

LARGE TASSELS

- Wrap around doorknobs
- Add to curtain tiebacks or furniture slipcover ties
- Hang from knobs on cabinetry or furniture as an accent
- Embellish the backs of dining chairs or chair covers

# terrific tassels

 Novelty yarns make more than comfy sweaters and throws. Use a single skein to fashion one or more tassels that resemble the pricey ones sold at upscale home decorating stores.

**1** Paint the topper as desired.

**2** Wrap the yarn around a book or VCR tape case until it is the desired fullness for your topper. The length and fullness will vary with the size of the topper. Slip an extra piece of yarn or a strand of perle cotton rope (see instructions *right* for making rope) under the top edge of the yarn hank. Tie it tightly to form the tassel.

**3** Slip a length of wire through the top opening in the tassel topper. Loop it through the tie of the tassel and back through the hole. Using the wire, pull the tassel up into the topper and pull the tie ends through the hole. Remove the wire and knot the tie ends several times to hold the tassel in the topper.

Leave the bottom ends looped, or cut through the loops to make strands. Further embellish the tassel and topper as desired.

## OPTIONAL EMBELLISHMENTS:

■ Glue extra yarn or perle cotton rope to the topper at natural breaks or along grooves.

■ Sew small beads to random strands of yarn.

■ Dangle crystals from the topper using thin wire. Using an awl, make two small holes on the inside of the lower edge of the topper. String a crystal onto thin wire and fold the wire into a U shape. Press the wire into the holes and glue it in place. Repeat for additional crystals.

■ Cover part or all of the topper with perle cotton. Brush a ¼-inch-wide band of glue onto the painted topper and tightly wrap the perle cotton over the glue. See the photograph *left* for details. Continue wrapping until the section is covered.

■ Make a pompom of matching yarn and tie it to the topper. Make the pompom in the same manner as the tassel bottom, leaving long tails when tying it off. Use the tails to tie the pompom around the topper. Trim the tails and clip the loops.

## making rope

To make perle cotton rope, use a yarn spinner and follow the manufacturer's directions. A hand or electric drill can also be used. To use a drill, loop one or more strands of perle cotton around a stationary object such as a doorknob or hook. Tie the perle cotton in place. Insert a hook in the drill (instead of a bit) and tie the loose ends of the perle cotton to the hook. NOTE: The more strands of perle cotton you use, the thicker the rope will be; colors can be mixed. Slowly turn the drill so the thread twists on itself to form a rope. Stop turning the drill when the rope is tight and does not untwist. Remove the ends from the doorknob or hook and the drill and tie them in an overhand knot.

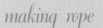

# a little light romance

Treat your friends to indulgences they admire but may never buy—a hanging lamp and etched bedside water pitcher.

## hanging 'round

A pretty bedside lamp fits anywhere an accent—or accent lighting—is needed. Beads and appliqués brighten plain organdy with color and personality.

Fold four 20-inch lengths of cord in half, creating loops. Attach them to the 2-inch macramé ring with an overhand loop, placing cords at the 12 o'clock, 3 o'clock, 6 o'clock, and 9 o'clock positions. See the photograph *above* for details.

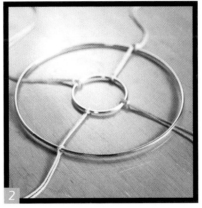

Center the 6-inch macramé ring over the 2-inch ring and tie the cords in the same manner. See the photograph *above* for placement details.

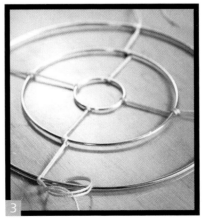

Repeat this process with the 10-inch ring. Pull cords as tightly as possible, checking that positions of all cords are equidistant.

4 Tie a knot on the outside of the 10-inch ring. Thread a bead through each pair of cord ends and tie another knot. Snip ends of four pairs of cords to desired length.

5 Cut a piece of organdy fabric into an 11½x20-inch rectangle. Sew the short ends together with a ⅜-inch seam allowance. Sew another seam ¼ inch away and clip excess fabric. Wrap one edge of the fabric tube over the 6-inch ring of the hanging structure and slip-stitch it in place. Sew other edge of fabric to another 6-inch ring in the same way. Both rings will be concealed.

6 Cut another rectangle of organdy fabric measuring 7x33½ inches. Make a second fabric tube and attach it to the two 10-inch rings in the manner described in Step 5. Sew beaded trim onto both bottom rings of lamp. Sew or glue appliquéd flowers to outside ring of organdy fabric. Attach a purchased hanging light fixture to the inside of the 2-inch ring.

137

138

## What You'll Need...

- Purchased water carafe with a drinking glass that fits as a lid
- Low-tack tape
- Stencil
- Etching cream
- Applicator sponge
- Disposable gloves
- 20-gauge wire
- Beads and jump rings

# glass etchings

An inexpensive water carafe and the cup that doubles as its lid exude an artistic air when etching and beads are added. Use a small purchased stencil and etching cream to create the patterns in the glassware.

**1** Thoroughly wash and dry the water carafe and drinking glass, making sure there are no traces of residue. Tape the stencil pattern onto front of pitcher.

Paint etching cream over the stencil following the manufacturer's directions. See the photograph *above* for details.

Rinse off the etching cream and remove the stencil. See the photograph *above* for details. Repeat the process around the pitcher and glass, taking care that the position of stencil is where you want it once glass is upside down on the pitcher.

**4** Wrap three strands of wire around the neck of the pitcher, leaving a long tail for each strand. Add beads to the tails.

## What You'll Need...

- ☐ 14½-inch square of heavy watercolor paper
- ☐ Gold watercolor paint
- ☐ Paintbrush
- ☐ 2 gold grommets
- ☐ 21 inches black wire
- ☐ Gold button and ribbon

# origami wall pockets

Folded paper pockets hold dried flowers, vintage photos, or even love notes.

**1** Fold the paper square according to the diagrams shown *below*.

**2** Paint a wavy gold line along the edges. See the photograph *right* for details.

**3** Set the grommets on either side of the upper flap, just above the folded edge.

**4** Fold the wire into a U shape. Turn the last 2 inches of each end at a right angle. Slide the wire through the grommets from back to front and curl the ends.

**5** Attach a gold button to the point of the pocket and tie ribbon to the handle.

139

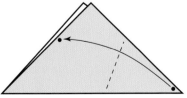

# heirloom display

A collage of old photos, buttons, trinkets, and "vintage" scrapbooking trims romanticize family history.

**1** Crop and trim the photocopies of your photographs. NOTE: Do not use actual photographs. Remove the frame's backing. Arrange the photographs on the backing; mark their placement. Remove the photos and arrange the paper background on the frame backing. Splice the paper so the cutting lines will be covered by the braid and the pattern of the paper aligns across the backing.

**2** Glue the papers to the backing using decoupage medium. Apply a light coat of decoupage medium over the paper. Let dry. Decoupage the photographs to the backing in the same manner.

**3** Position the braid over the splices in the background paper and tack it in place with hot glue. Arrange the other decorative items on the collage and glue them in place.

**4** String the beads and pearls onto wire, add the letter beads, and finish with more beads and pearls. Turn under and crimp the wire ends to secure the bead strand. Slip the ends under the bands of braid and hot-glue them in place. Reassemble the frame, backing, and glass.

Share old memories or make room for new ones with a photo collage or scrapbook. **thanks**

## What You'll Need...

- Purchased scrapbook measuring approximately 12×12 inches
- Crafts knife
- Mat board to fit the scrapbook front
- Coordinating lightweight fabrics 2 inches larger than the scrapbook
- Tacky crafts glue
- Clip-style clothespins
- Wide grosgrain ribbon
- Narrow ribbon or braid
- Additional fabric for the inside lining

# picture window

Personalize a purchased scrapbook with fabric and a cutout window that gives a hint at what's inside.

1 Disassemble the scrapbook and work with only the front and back covers. Cut mat board to fit the front of the scrapbook minus any hinge sections that turn back.

2 Cut a window in the lower right corner of the mat board. The window shown measures 4×3½ inches and is positioned 2½ inches from each edge.

Lay the main fabric face down and center the mat board over it, right side down. Wrap the fabric to the back of the mat board. Working from the corners in and mitering as you go, glue the fabric to the wrong side of the mat board. Use clothespins to hold the fabric in place until the glue dries completely.

3 To make the window, cut an X in the fabric from corner to corner of the window. Pull the fabric triangles through the window and to the back of the mat board. Glue it in place and secure with clothespins until the glue dries.

4 Weave grosgrain ribbon over the covered mat board and glue it in place.

Glue narrow ribbon around the window. See the photograph *above* for details.

5 Cover the scrapbook front and back in the same manner, omitting the mat board and covering the entire piece—including any hinge sections that turn back.

6 Glue the window mat to the scrapbook front, leaving an opening for inserting the photograph between the two layers. Hold the two layers together with clothespins and let dry overnight.

7 Add narrow ribbon to the outer edge of the front cover. To finish the inside of the covers, cut fabric the same size as the cover. Press under ½ inch all around. Glue the fabric to the inside, concealing all raw edges. Reassemble the scrapbook.

# for the memories

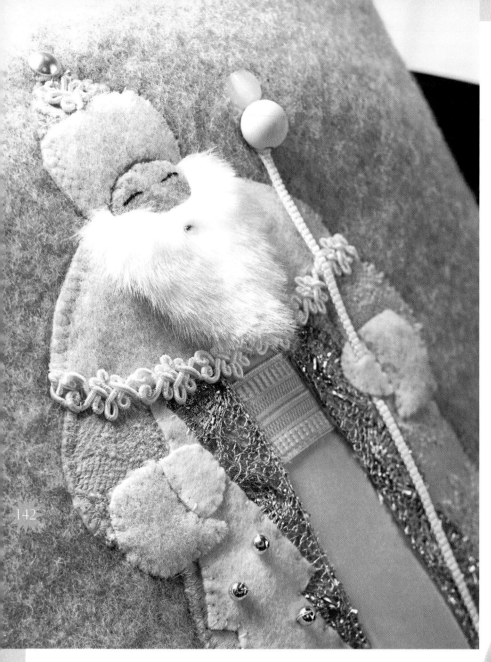

1 NOTE: All appliqué is done first on muslin, then transferred to the pillow top fabric. Enlarge the patterns on *page 156* and transfer them to muslin. Cut out all the appliqué pieces from the appropriate fabrics and trims.

2 Embroider the face pieces. Baste the coat, dress, hand, and face pieces onto the muslin. Cut out the designs and baste them to the centers of the pillow fronts.

3 Starting from the bottom and working up, overlay and baste the remaining pieces in place. See the photographs *left* and *opposite* for details. Hand-stitch or use a sewing machine to zigzag-stitch them in place. Do not sew the outer edges to the blue wool until the design is complete.

# old world charmers

**Whether you know them** as Grandfather Frost and The Snow Maiden or by any other name, these European-inspired appliqué figures are cloaked in rich, elegant fabrics and finished with fine detail.

## What You'll Need...

**FOR BOTH FIGURES:**
- [ ] Natural muslin
- [ ] White artificial fur
- [ ] Red (mouth) and black (eyes) quilter's thread
- [ ] Powder rouge or blush for the cheeks
- [ ] Fabric glue

**FOR GRANDFATHER FROST:**
- [ ] White and ivory wool felt
- [ ] Pink and ivory wool fabric
- [ ] White satin for the robe
- [ ] Light tan satin brocade for the cloak
- [ ] Small fancy white trim for the cape
- [ ] ³⁄₄-inch-wide silver lace
- [ ] ¹⁄₄-inch pearl or button for the hat
- [ ] Twenty ¹⁄₄-inch silver beads for tree trim
- [ ] Narrow flat white braid for the staff
- [ ] ¹⁄₂-inch ivory bead and oval bead for the staff top

**FOR THE SNOW MAIDEN:**
- [ ] Ivory wool felt for the hat and sleeves
- [ ] Ivory wool for the coat
- [ ] White lace for the sleeve and headpiece overlays
- [ ] Small fancy trim for the dress front
- [ ] Large ivory trim for the outer headpiece overlay
- [ ] ³⁄₄-inch-wide silver lace
- [ ] Seven ¹⁄₄-inch pearls for the headpiece
- [ ] Flat silver braid for the headpiece streamers
- [ ] Flat ecru braid for the headband and cuffs
- [ ] Red seed beads for the mouth
- [ ] Tiny seed pearls for the headband

**FOR THE PILLOWS:**
- [ ] 18×20-inch piece of blue wool for the front
- [ ] 18×20-inch piece of blue cotton for the back
- [ ] Polyester fiberfill

143

4 Embroider the mouth on the beard and glue the beard to Grandfather Frost's face. Cut a ¹⁄₄-inch-wide strip of fur for the Maiden's dress hem and collar; glue it in place.

5 Glue on all remaining laces and braids, except for the staffs. Sew on all the beads and pearls, except those for the staff. Hand-sew or zigzag-stitch the outer edges to the pillow. If necessary, use glue in difficult spots. Remove all basting. Apply rouge to the cheeks. Glue the staff in place and sew the beads over the staff end.

6 Using ¹⁄₂-inch seams, with right sides matching, sew the fronts to the backs. Leave an opening for turning and stuffing. Stuff the pillow tightly and sew the opening closed.

In the Cards: Recycle old Christmas cards and use them to piece together a decoupage collage. Cut or punch large squares from coordinating cards, then decoupage them onto a tray you've painted to match. Decoupage a full card in the center, then top the card with circles of plain paper enhanced with rub-on letters to spell out your seasonal wish. Seal the tray with two more coats of decoupage medium.

Top it Off: Package toppers abound in gifts and crafts stores. Turn these inexpensive trinkets, holiday buttons, or miniatures into instant jewelry. Remove any wires, ties, or findings, then glue pin or earring backs to them using industrial-strength glue.

# In a Twinkling:
# gifts to give

Pick a Pocket: Add a pocket vase to a purchased frame for a romantic touch. Shape the vase from polymer clay. If you want a tassel of beads, make a hole in the clay and thread a jump ring through the hole. Bake the clay according to the manufacturer's instructions. Paint the frame and vase, then glue the vase to the frame with industrial-strength glue. Add beads to the jump ring. Use only artificial flowers in the vase; it will not be watertight.

◀ Shaker Style: Give new life to odd-lot vintage or replica salt and pepper shakers by turning them into picture holders. Using needlenose pliers, coil the end of a strand of 18-gauge florist's wire for the spiral holders or wrap it around a dowel for the circular holders. Trim the wire to the desired length and slip the straight end through a hole in the shaker lid. Leave the shaker empty or fill with salt or colored sugar if weight is needed.

▲ Stick With It: Turn plain pillar candles into nostalgic accents simply by adding stickers. Choose purchased stickers with a clear backing or print your own using clip art and clear matte label paper. Trim away the excess margin and smooth the sticker onto the side of the candle. NOTE: Use this technique only on large pillar candles that do not melt around the outer shell. Never leave burning candles unattended.

◀ Mix and Match: C'mon baby light my fire using matches from a wintry matchbox (available at crafts stores). Paint a purchased box, then glue precut painted trees around the sides and stars to the top. For the knob, stack and glue two stars together. Using an old toothbrush and white paint, splatter-paint the box for a blizzard of fun. If desired, glue a strip of emery paper to the bottom for striking.

It's the kids who

# make holidays special for most of us.

Join in their excitement by making gifts for the children in your life—or for anyone who is a child at heart. The featured projects are simple enough so everyone in the family can enjoy the fun of creating.

JUST *for* KIDS

# soap stars

Bring sparkle to a kids' bathroom with star-studded accessories. Polymer clay is applied directly to purchased ceramic pieces, then baked to a hard finish.

## FOR THE BATH SET:

1 Remove any stickers and plastic pieces from the bath set. Wipe the surface with rubbing alcohol. Cut paper strips for patterns to go around each piece. Enlarge the star pattern on *page 157* to scale and transfer to paper.

2 Place freezer paper, slick side down, on your work surface. Following the manufacturer's directions, roll out the clay. Using the patterns for length and using a crafts knife, cut 3/4-inch-wide red strips, 1/2-inch-wide blue strips, and 1/4-inch-wide green strips. Cut stars from yellow clay. Roll out small balls from yellow and red.

3 Layer the red, blue, and green strips for each piece. Place three red balls on each star. Evenly space the stars along each band. Add yellow balls between the stars.

4 Wrap each strip around the base of the corresponding piece. Lightly press the extending star tips to the ceramic piece to avoid breakage.

5 If desired, roll out medium-size yellow and red balls for towel trim. Slide the balls onto the wire for baking.

Place all the items on a baking sheet lined with foil. Bake according to the manufacturer's directions. After the clay has cooled, seal it with satin glaze. Let dry.

## FOR THE TOWEL:

1 Separately prewash and dry the towel, felt, and ribbons.

2 Cut the blue ribbon to fit across the band of the towel, adding 1/4-inch extra to each end for turning under. Fuse under the ends, then fuse the ribbon to the towel following the manufacturer's directions. Repeat for the green ribbon, centering it over the blue. Tack the ends in place.

3 Cut a star from the yellow felt and fuse it to the center of the ribbon bands. Hand-sew around the star edges. Sew three red balls or buttons to the star. Sew the yellow balls or buttons along the remainder of the band.

# bright patches

Kids and color go together like crayons and paper. Mix together snippets of fun fabrics for quick and easy projects that are jumping with color and pattern.

150

## pack it up

 Strips of playful colors and patterns line up as stripes on a drawstring backpack that's perfect for overnights, dance and sports clothes, or toting toys to a friend's house.

**1** Cut the fabric into 26×3-inch strips on the crosswise grain. Arrange the strips in the desired order. Sew them together lengthwise using ½-inch seam allowances. Zigzag or surge the seam allowances and the raw edge to prevent fraying.

**2** Press under ½ inch along the side edges. Fuse the edges in place. Fold the bag in half crosswise, wrong sides facing. Create a pleat at the bottom of the bag by folding up ½ inch on each side, forming a W at the bottom.

**3** Starting at the top edge, sew the sides together by edgestitching the front to the back along the long edges. Stop the stitching 1 inch down from the top and resume it ¾ inch later. This will leave an opening for the drawstring.

**4** To form the upper casing, turn the raw edge under 1 inch. Topstitch around the upper edge ¾ inch from the folded edge. Reinforce the stitching at the openings.

**5** Place a grommet at each lower corner following the package instructions and going through all layers of fabric. Cut the cord in half. Starting at one side of the casing, feed one cord through the casing. Turn back and feed the cord through the other side of the casing, forming a loop. Pull the cord halfway through the casings. Bring both ends to the bottom, and thread one cord through the grommet. See the photograph *above* for details. Repeat with the other cord, going in the opposite direction. Have the child try on the backpack. Adjust the cords as needed and knot them in place at the grommet; trim the ends. To draw up the cord, pull each side.

152

What You'll Need...

- [ ] Paper or cardboard for templates
- [ ] Fabric marker
- [ ] 4 colors of felt
- [ ] Matching thread
- [ ] Polyester fiberfill
- [ ] Perle cotton in one or more matching colors
- [ ] Large-eyed needle
- [ ] 5 coordinating buttons

# starring parts

Triangles and a pentagon button up to warm your rooms with bright appeal during the holidays or all year long.

**1** Enlarge the pattern on *page 157* to scale and transfer it to paper or cardboard. Trace around the templates onto doubled thicknesses of the desired colors of felt.

**2** Cut out all the pieces. For the triangles, topstitch the long edges and leave the short edge open. For the pentagon, leave a small opening on one side. Stuff each piece lightly and topstitch the opening closed.

**3** Lay the pentagon over the triangles so the seams overlap.

**4** Using long strands of perle cotton and a single stitch, sew a button at each point of the pentagon, joining all the pieces. Knot the perle cotton to hold the buttons in place and trim the ends.

What You'll Need...

- Paper for patterns
- Felt in the desired colors
- Fabric glue
- Embroidery floss in contrasting colors
- Embroidery needle
- Assorted buttons and charms including a star-shape button
- 8-inch length of ¼-inch-wide ribbon
- Polyester fiberfill

# crazy quilting

❧ Easy felt ornaments mimic the charm of old-fashioned crazy quilts. Glue actually holds them together—the stitching is simply decorative.

1 Enlarge the patterns on *page 157* to scale and transfer all the pieces to paper; cut out the pattern pieces.

2 For each ornament, cut two full pieces for the background. Cut all of the patchwork pieces from other scraps. Arrange the patchwork pieces on one background piece so there are no gaps. Glue the patchwork pieces in place.

3 Using three plies of embroidery floss and the desired stitches, sew over the seams. Sew around the outer edge with long running stitches. Sew all the buttons and charms except the star button to the patchwork pieces.

4 Place the patchwork piece over the remaining background piece with wrong sides facing. Fold the ribbon in half for a hanger and slip the ends between the pieces. Sew around the edges using a blanket stitch or other desired stitches. Leave an opening for stuffing. Lightly stuff the ornament and continue stitching it closed. Sew the star button at the base of the ribbon.

# pet power

Whether you consider it to be doggone cute or the cat's meow, a pet-themed table and chairs will be a howling hit for your little ones.

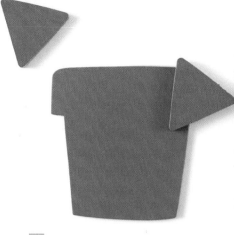

3 To make the dog face, lay triangles over the flowerpot rims for the ears. See the photograph *above* for details. Cut lengths of gray floss for eyebrows and mustache and glue them in place. After the glue dries, fray the ends. Glue the eyes and nose in place. Glue the dog face to the back of the dog chair.

1 Sand the furniture and wipe it clean. Prime and paint it, sanding lightly between coats. Spray-paint the letters the desired colors, the bones tan, the teardrop mice gray, and the face shapes the desired colors. NOTE: You can substitute acrylic paint for spray paint. Paint the eyes and noses the desired colors.

2 On each table leg, glue *BOW WOW* down one outside edge and *MEOW MEOW* down the other outside edge. Glue the same words on the backs of the chairs.

4 For the cat face, glue triangles over the upper lobes of the heart for ears. See the photograph *above* for details. Cut lengths of white floss for whiskers and glue them in place. After the glue dries, fray the ends. Glue the eyes and nose in place and glue the cat face to the back of the cat chair.

5 Glue pairs of bones together, sandwiching ribbon between them. Glue pairs of teardrops together, sandwiching floss tails and ribbon between them. Make black dot eyes on the mice. Staple the ribbons to the inside apron of the chair backs and on opposing sides of the inside table apron, knotting the ends if needed. See the photograph *opposite* for details.

## variations on a theme

If your child doesn't dig dogs and cats, use techniques and materials similar to those described to create custom furniture for almost any other interest. Paint the furniture as desired. Check crafts stores for precut shapes that can be attached to the furniture. For unusual shapes, piece together basics like triangles, rectangles, and circles. Look for wooden shapes and garlands you can string or dangle.

For the Christmas chair shown *above*, paint geometric and Christmas patterns onto the chair. Glue painted wooden stars to the upper corners and snowmen between the back rungs. Thread painted Christmas shapes onto yarn and tie them to the lowest rung of the chair back.

155

6 Using the black paint pen, draw stylized paw prints on the table and chair aprons. Using other colors, write pet-related words across the tabletop.

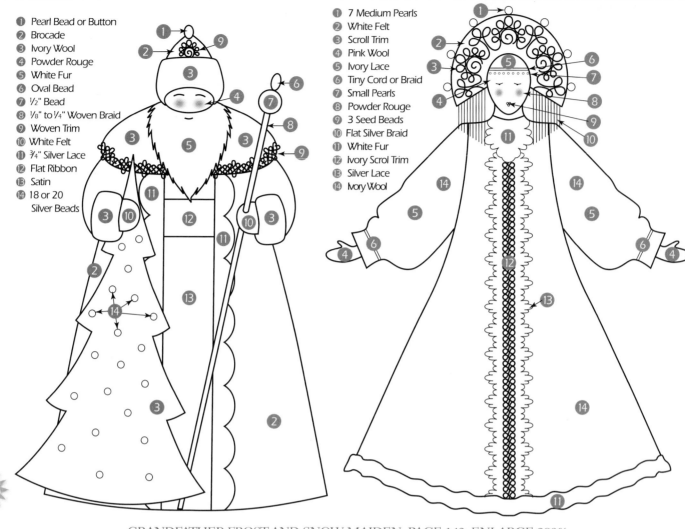

1. Pearl Bead or Button
2. Brocade
3. Ivory Wool
4. Powder Rouge
5. White Fur
6. Oval Bead
7. ½" Bead
8. ⅛" to ¼" Woven Braid
9. Woven Trim
10. White Felt
11. ¾" Silver Lace
12. Flat Ribbon
13. Satin
14. 18 or 20 Silver Beads

1. 7 Medium Pearls
2. White Felt
3. Scroll Trim
4. Pink Wool
5. Ivory Lace
6. Tiny Cord or Braid
7. Small Pearls
8. Powder Rouge
9. 3 Seed Beads
10. Flat Silver Braid
11. White Fur
12. Ivory Scrol Trim
13. Silver Lace
14. Ivory Wool

GRANDFATHER FROST AND SNOW MAIDEN, PAGE 142; ENLARGE 280%

ORNAMENTAL TOTE, PAGE 124; ENLARGE 200%

LEAFY TABLEAU, PAGE 16;
ENLARGE TABLE LEAVES TO WIDTH OF RUNNER;
ENLARGE NAPKIN TIES 260%

For mulled wine or cider, empty contents of one mix into saucepan; add one 750-ml bottle fruity red wine or 1 quart apple cider. Bring to boiling; reduce heat. Simmer, uncovered, 30 minutes. If using wine, stir in 2 tablespoons sugar until dissolved. Strain mixture, discarding solids. Serve warm.

TAG AND INSTRUCTIONS FOR
MULLED WINE OR CIDER SPICE
MIX, PAGE 114

TAB PLACEMENT

TAB
Cut 2
on fold

BOOT 1
Cut 2

fold

CUFF
Cut 1
on fold

BOOT 2
Cut 2

fold

BOOT 3
Cut 2

STAR OF DAVID BOBECHE,
CONFETTI, & GIFT TAG

WHAT A KICK, PAGE 32; ENLARGE TO
MEASURE 18, 14, AND 23 INCHES, 775%

STAR LIGHT, STAR BRIGHT,
PAGE 61; ENLARGE BOBECHE
250%, CONFETTI 150%. GIFT
POUCH TAG 120%

FLOWER POWER
Cut 4

DANCING STARS
Cut 5 each size

SOAP
STARS

FLOWER POWER, PAGE 126;
ENLARGE 165%

DANCING STARS,
PAGE 38, ENLARGE
200%,150%,
AND 125%

SOAP STARS,
PAGE 148;
ENLARGE 200%
FOR TOWEL

157

STARRING PARTS,
PAGE 152;
ENLARGE 340%

C
Cut 2

Cut 1

Cut 1

B
B

A
A

A
A

CENTER
Cut 1

C
C

MAKING MUSIC, PAGE 84;
ENLARGE NOTES
AND TOPPER
280%, ENLARGE
TREBLE CLEF
FOR WREATH TO
14 INCHES, 560%

LIGHTEN UP,
PAGE 12

CRAZY QUILTING, PAGE 153; ENLARGE 225%

# credits & sources

**Unless otherwise stated, photo styling by Marisa Dirks and Jilann Severson.**
**Food styling by Charles Worthington. Photographs by Jay Wilde.**

**cover, page 4:** ornament display box design, Marisa Dirks

**pages 8–13:** designs, Suzi Carson

**page 14:** design, Jilann Severson

**pages 16–17:** designs, Marisa Dirks

**pages 18–19:** Line Lights centerpiece design, Jilann Severson; Fall Wraps design, Carol Linnan

**pages 20–23:** designs, Jim Williams; photographs, Tria Giovan

**pages 26–31:** designs, Joann Brantley

**pages 32–33:** designs, Brian Carter

**pages 34–37:** designs, Jim Williams; photographs, Tria Giovan

**page 38:** design, Suzi Carson

**page 39:** design, Sharon Widdop

**pages 40–41:** Simple Greeting design, Marisa Dirks; A Light Touch design adaptation, Carol Linnan

**pages 42–45:** designs, Talathy O'Sullivan; photographs, Tria Giovan

**pages 46–47:** designs, Marisa Dirks

**pages 50–51:** Lucky Breaks design, Joann Brantley; Tree Ornament design, Marisa Dirks

**pages 54–59:** designs, Jim Williams

**pages 60–61:** designs, Mary Jo Hiney

**pages 62–63:** Christmas 2 #6MC571 decoupage paper by Mignon Clift available through MaryJean Online at www.maryjeanonline.com or call 1/800-678-4178

**pages 64–69:** Roast Duckling with Maple-Cider Glaze, Green Beans with Carrots and Citrus-Hazelnut Gremolata, and Potato Brie Gratin recipes developed by Colleen Weeden; Citrus-Tapenade Game Hens recipe developed by Ellen Boeke

**pages 70–77:** Smoked Salmon Pasta Bake, Rustic Gremolata Potatoes, Roasted Vegetable Phyllo Bake, Croque Monsieur Triangles, Lime Pecan Shortbread Bars, and Orzo-Shrimp Salad recipes developed by Ellen Boeke

**pages 78–85:** Garlicky Marinated Vegetables, Chocolate Chai, Four-Cheese Spread, Mini- and White-Chocolate Cheesecakes recipes developed by Colleen Weeden; project and decorating designs, Gayle Schadendorf; Fiskars Elegance Border Punch #23447097 available at crafts and scrapbooking stores nationwide or contact Fiskars Brands, Inc. at www.fiskars.com or call 1/866-348-5661

**page 88:** Raspberry and White Chocolate Dacquoise recipe developed by Ellen Boeke

**page 92:** Lemon-Almond Cake Roll recipe developed by Colleen Weeden

**pages 94–103:** Maple-Dijon Salmon Bites, Artichoke Caponata, Shrimp Crostini with Chimichurri Sauce, Chicken Drummettes with Plum Sauce, Lamb Pita Chips with Garlic-Yogurt Sauce recipes developed by Ellen Boeke; project and decorating designs, Gayle Schadendorf

**pages 110–113:** Easy Layered Fudge (page 112) recipe developed by Colleen Weeden; candy box designs, Jim Williams

**page 116–119:** Cured Olives and Manchego Cheese; Cava Granada Cocktail; Spanish Omelet with Potato, Spanish Onion and Serrano Ham; Orange, Red Grape, and Watercress Salad; and Almond-Hazelnut Cookies recipes developed by Joyce Lock

**pages 122–123:** designs, Jilann Severson

**pages 124–125:** designs, Jilann Severson

**pages 126–127:** designs, Marisa Dirks

**pages 128–129:** designs, Marisa Dirks

**pages 130–131:** designs, Kristin Detrick

**pages 132–133:** designs, Jilann Severson

**pages 134–135:** designs, Gayle Schadendorf; Create a Tassel toppers available at crafts stores or contact Toner Plastics, www.tonerplastics.com or call 1/800-723-1792; Caron Jewel Box chenille yarn, Emerald 0009 available at crafts and needlework stores nationwide or contact Caron Yarns at www.caron.com; Lion Brand ribbon yarn, Autumn Leaves #520 color 206 and Lion Brand chenille yarn #108 Dusty Blue Chenille available at crafts and needlework stores nationwide or contact Lion Brand Yarn at www.lionbrand.com or call 1/800-258-9276

**pages 136–138:** designs, Marisa Dirks

**page 139:** designs, Suzi Carson

**page 140:** design, Carol Linnan

**page 141:** design, Gayle Schadendorf

**pages 142–143:** designs, Suzi Carson

**pages 144–145:** In the Cards tray design, Marisa Dirks; Mix and Match matchbox design, Jilann Severson; Top it Off jewelry designs, Jilann Severson; Pick a Pocket frame design, Kristin Detrick

**pages 148–149:** designs, Kristin Detrick; photographs, Marty Baldwin

**pages 150–151:** backpack designs, Gayle Schadendorf

**pages 154–155:** designs, Jilann Severson

# index

# index *continued*